HUMANIZE YOUR BRAND

MARIAM FARAG

PASSIONPRENEUR®
P U B L I S H I N G

HUMANIZE YOUR BRAND

Stand Out in a Busy Digital World

MARIAM FARAG

PASSIONPRENEUR® PUBLISHING

Publishing information
Publishing and design facilitated by Passionpreneur Publishing
A division of Passionpreneur Organization Pty Ltd
ABN: 48640637529

Melbourne, VIC | Australia
www.passionpreneurpublishing.com

To my mother, whose unwavering love and
support have been my anchor and my inspiration.
Your endless sacrifices and wisdom have
guided me through the toughest of times.

To my boys, who fill my life with joy and purpose.
You remind me daily of the beauty in every moment
and inspire me to strive for a better future.

To the countless individuals who have inspired and
contributed to my growth, both personally and
professionally. Your influence has been invaluable on
this journey, and I am forever grateful for the lessons
learned and the encouragement received.

ACKNOWLEDGEMENTS

To all the wonderful people who played a part in the creation of this book:

This book wouldn't exist without your steadfast support and guidance. A special thanks to my incredible book coach Shobha, who pushed me to reach my writing goals and helped me overcome every obstacle. And to the individuals who have inspired me throughout my personal and professional life, your influence has been invaluable.

Thank you to every person who has contributed to my professional experience, taught me how to rise above the occasion, and trusted me with their personal brands, impact, and stories. Thank you from the bottom of my heart.

TABLE OF CONTENTS

Chapter 12
HUMANIZING BRANDS

INTRODUCTION

In the Digital Age, where brands are constantly vying for attention, humanizing brands has become more important than ever. By forging authentic connections with their audience, brands can establish trust, loyalty, and advocacy. In this book, we will explore the concept of humanizing brands, understand its significance, and provide practical strategies for both organizational and personal brand humanization.

CHAPTER 1

THE POWER OF HUMAN CONNECTIONS

Humanizing Brands in the Modern Era

Throughout my life, being judged by my appearance was a recurring theme that deeply affected my emotional wellbeing. This superficial evaluation by others became a mirror through which I viewed myself, leading to years of internalizing negative perceptions and battling with self-esteem. However, the journey from that point of vulnerability to where I stand now has been one of profound growth, introspection, and discovery.

Since the age of 14, I've been acutely aware of the 'why' of my life—a desire to create a meaningful impact and touch people's lives in a profound way. This purpose was born out of my unique family dynamics, particularly growing up without my father's presence. This absence could have been a source of despair, but instead became a wellspring of motivation, largely thanks to the strongest influence in my life—my mother. A resilient businesswoman, she was not just a parent but also a living testament to the power of determination, strength, and self-worth.

From her, I learned invaluable lessons about the importance of knowing your worth and the necessity of standing up for yourself. In a society that often prioritizes appearances over substance, my mother's example was a beacon of truth. She demonstrated that true value doesn't come from external validation, but instead from understanding and embracing your own worth.

A TURBULENT PATH LED TO RESILIENT PURSUITS

The path to this realization was not straightforward. It was laden with challenges, moments of self-doubt, and instances where the world's superficial judgments seemed insurmountable. Yet it was through these very struggles that I found clarity and strength. I began to see that my worth was not tied to how others perceived me. It was inherently linked to the impact I could make and the lives I could touch.

This understanding did not emerge in isolation. It was the culmination of various key moments and realizations. One pivotal moment was when I decided to channel my experiences and emotions into helping others. I recognized that my journey equipped me with unique insights and empathy towards those facing similar challenges. My mission became clear: to use my voice and experiences to inspire and empower others.

Embracing my worth, and understanding what I bring to the table, transformed my approach to life. It taught me that standing up for oneself is not just about asserting your value in the face of doubt, but also about living in a way that reflects your deep-seated beliefs and values. It's about walking the talk, embodying your worth in every action, and letting your life's work speak for itself.

This transformation is the cornerstone of my message and the essence of my book. It's a testament to the journey from being judged by appearances to achieving a state of self-assuredness, purpose, and impact. My narrative is not just about overcoming personal challenges; it's also a call to action for others to recognize their worth, stand firm in their values, and make a tangible difference in the world.

The Journey Begins

In sharing my story, I aim to bridge the gap between personal struggle and universal truths. I want to show that the journey to self-discovery and impact is not reserved for a select few but is accessible to anyone willing to confront their challenges and embrace their true worth. Through my book, I hope to inspire others to navigate their paths with courage, determination, and the knowledge that their value extends far beyond the superficial judgments of the world.

My journey was a winding path marked by judgment, self-doubt, and the relentless quest for identity. These experiences, though fraught with challenge, became the bedrock upon which I would build my understanding of personal branding and storytelling.

'Aha' Moments: Discovering My Voice

Realizing what I wanted to say was a journey of countless trials, errors, and revelations. Initially, my voice felt lost in the cacophony of external expectations and self-imposed limitations. The turning point came through a series of 'aha' moments that illuminated the power of authentic expression. Learning when to speak and when to embrace silence taught me the subtleties of impactful communication. Each moment of realization was a step towards understanding the nuanced dance taking place between speaking one's truth and listening to the world's rhythms.

THE POWER OF EMOTIONAL INTELLIGENCE (EQ)

Embracing emotional intelligence was a transformative aspect. It wasn't merely about being aware of my emotions, as it also involved understanding the emotions of those around me. This realization dawned on me as I navigated the complexities of interpersonal dynamics without the guidance of traditional mentors. Instead, I found wisdom in the lived experiences of others, drawing lessons from their resilience and adaptability. These insights were instrumental in refining my voice, enabling me to connect on a deeper, more empathetic level.

Realizing the Power of Personal Branding

The concept of personal branding evolved from a theoretical understanding to a lived experience. It became clear that personal branding is *not* about self-promotion; instead, it's about authenticity and the value one brings to every interaction. Sharing my experience was the first step in this journey, because this act of vulnerability transformed my perception of branding. My personal story, with its ups and downs, became a powerful tool for connection, making me a magnetic presence in my industry.

Transformation Through Vulnerability

This journey of self-discovery and branding brought about a profound personal transformation. I learned the importance of humility over arrogance, understanding that true strength lies in acknowledging one's vulnerabilities. Turning pain into power, I embraced my past, using it as a foundation for growth and a source of inspiration for others. This shift wasn't just internal; it manifested in tangible results in my life and business, enhancing my impact and broadening my reach.

Advocating for Mental Health

My advocacy is a crucial aspect of my personal and professional identity. Sharing my story has not only been cathartic but has also opened up conversations around mental health, challenging stigma and promoting understanding. This advocacy is a reflection of my commitment to using my platform for creating societal impact, demonstrating the power of personal branding in driving meaningful change.

WHY MY STORY MATTERS

My narrative is more than a personal account; it's also a testament to the transformative power of storytelling and branding. Through my experiences, I aim to demonstrate that embracing one's story can lead to genuine connections, opportunities, and influence. My journey underscores the importance of authenticity in establishing a resonant and enduring brand. It's a message of empowerment, encouraging others to own their stories and use them as a force for impact.

The Expertise Behind the Narrative

My expertise is rooted in real-world experiences, shaped by the lessons learned through overcoming adversity. From advocating for mental health to empowering others through personal branding, my journey exemplifies the power of resilience and the impact of authenticity. These experiences, combined with my professional accomplishments, establish my credibility and underscore my message's authenticity.

Social Proof of Impact

The true measure of my approach's success lies in the stories of those I've helped. From individuals finding their voice to organizations redefining their branding strategies, my work has facilitated transformations that echo my own journey. These success stories serve as social proof of the efficacy of authentic storytelling and personal branding, illustrating the profound impact these principles can have when applied with intention and integrity.

The Power of Personal Branding and Authentic Storytelling

The journey from being judged on appearances to becoming an authentic authority in my field has been both challenging and rewarding. It has taught me that personal branding and storytelling are not just about career advancement but also about living a life of purpose and impact. By embracing my story and the lessons it contains, I've been able to connect, inspire, and influence in ways I never thought possible.

Going Forward

I invite you to journey through the pages of this book, where you will discover not just theories but also real-life stories, insights, and strategies that have propelled industry leaders to success. This book is more than a guide; it's a blueprint for those aspiring to cultivate an authentic personal reputation while leading with purpose.

Whether you're seeking to redefine your brand, enhance your leadership presence, or leave a meaningful legacy in your field, this book is your key to unlocking the full potential of your brand and securing your place at the top of your game. Let's embark on the journey of transforming your vision into impactful reality together.

CHAPTER 2

THE POWER IN BRANDING AND STORYTELLING

Creating Authentic Connections
in the Digital Age

If you were to disappear, or your brand ceased to exist today, what would consumers say about you? Would they even *remember* you ... and if so, how? This isn't just about being memorable—it's about creating a lasting impact through the connections and impressions you've made. In today's Digital Age, this has become not just an aspiration but a *necessity*.

What would you like to be remembered by?

To successfully build a memorable presence, brands need to change how they market their products, convey their visions and their values, and communicate with the public. All three facets have become a key part of building a brand.

Whether it's through customer relations, product placement, or public communication, your brand is being *judged*.

To better understand this reality, let's zoom in on personal branding and examine how it's the key to staying relevant. (It's now so important, in fact, that if you lack a marketing strategy, your brand will simply vanish in the crowded marketplace.)

Whether you're a 12-year-old athlete or a 50-year-old C-suite executive, personal branding comes in different stages and phases. It doesn't start with a job. It starts with you, an individual, defining your mission in life. In short, it's your 'why'.

In the Digital Age, social media plays a huge role in everyone's definition of relevance. With this in mind, we need to think very carefully about what we post, because it lives forever.

In addition, how we portray ourselves, how we represent our brand, and how we define our persona are key elements of building a special value point. *Everyone* should have a persona—a unique identity which remains consistent over time.

In this book, we'll cover how to create your own persona. We'll then delve into how you can stay true to it, whether you're a big brand, a corporation, or an individual. Given our incredibly crowded marketplace, understanding exactly how to do this has never been more important.

BRANDING IS NO LONGER A LUXURY—IT'S A NECESSITY

Just as your fingerprints are unique, *you* are unique. Yet unfortunately, if nobody's aware of your special qualities and offerings, you'll simply ... disappear.

Look at the world we now live in. It's all online. Our social media environment's completely saturated with people who just want to *be* someone, whether they have a message worth sharing or any influence over others. With everyone wanting to be anyone, and anyone wanting to be everyone, standing out is imperative. If you fail to do this, you've got no chance of hitting your target.

Whether you're a boutique agency, a corporation, or a personal brand, you share this need for uniqueness. Otherwise, you'll simply be lost in translation, swamped by the endless deluge of content out there. In the Digital Age, where brands are constantly vying for attention, humanizing brands has become more important than ever. By forging authentic connections with their audience, brands can establish trust, loyalty, and advocacy.

In *Humanize Your Brand*, we'll address this issue by exploring the concept of making your brand's essence more emotionally resonant, understanding this concept's unprecedented significance, and providing practical strategies for both organizational and personal brand humanization.

This book is focused on two things:

1. How corporations can communicate with purpose, truly authenticating their storytelling and service by becoming more customer-centric.
2. How you can create a powerful personal brand by showing the world that you're unique as a person. Instead of simply throwing out information, you'll learn how to take your brand to the next level by authentically standing out while keeping your objectives real.

In today's rapidly evolving digital marketplace, the tendency to emphasize sales numbers without considering the human element behind the brand is a significant misconception that many businesses still harbor. Some might dismiss the human-centric approach as mere fluff, questioning its relevance in the face of direct sales strategies.

We'll explore practical strategies for integrating a human-centric approach into every facet of your business, from the way you present yourself and interact with customers to how you engage with vendors and embody your values through public speaking and leadership.

In the process, you'll grasp the essence of what sets us apart from machines—namely, our ability to connect, empathize, and communicate authentically. Through real-world examples and actionable insights, you'll discover how to infuse your brand and leadership with a human touch, making your mark in the industry and leaving a lasting impression on your audience.

Keeping it Real

By the time you've reached the conclusion, you'll understand why humanizing brands is the key to success. You'll discover how forging stronger connections with customers helps your business. You'll realize that differentiating yourself from competitors will increase engagement while building trust. And while learning these things, you'll develop a shockproof crisis management strategy to ensure the trust you've so carefully built up is maintained in the most challenging circumstances.

Whether you're an individual or an entity, how you present yourself, integrate this image within your business's DNA, and handle your vendors is interconnected with your unique brand.

Senior leaders of large organizations routinely build trust and connectivity with their audience by telling them exactly what they stand for. In the following chapters, we'll further explore how to practically apply these principles to your own brand strategy. To do this, we'll break down the processes required to create engaging digital experiences, navigate the digital landscape's abundant challenges, and leverage personal narratives to build credibility, trust, and transparency.

Humanizing your brand is not merely a 'nice to have' or a one-off PR stunt; it's a vital strategy for differentiation and building long-lasting relationships with your customers. It's about moving beyond transactional interactions to create genuine human-to-human connections. It's time to debunk the myth that human-centric branding is secondary to direct sales tactics. By understanding the value of humanizing your brand, you will learn how to truly stand out in a crowded market, turning casual customers into loyal advocates and fundamentally transforming the way your brand is perceived.

The Modern Ecosystem Offers Many Options

In the old days, communication levels were low in comparison to today, with brand-building more about press releases and straightforward marketing than telling a story. Thankfully, these times of fluff and fancy words are over. With the world now well-stocked with easily accessible information, anyone can sniff out a fake piece of advertising. In this era, value is created by building authentic connections while communicating your brand's unique story.

Advertising is no longer a one-size-fits-all industry. To speak effectively with the customer, you need to carefully choose your criteria and mode of communication. For example, if you're running a global campaign, it's essential to *localize* it. To do this effectively, you'll need to speak to the local people and strive to understand their culture and traditions. Start by providing a survey with a range of meaningful, open-ended questions, including:

- What resonates with you emotionally?
- What characteristics do you trust in a brand?
- Whom do you see as credible?
- How can you make it clear that you are accountable for your words?

Customers are extremely well-informed, with access to a wide range of information through social media. For this reason, achieving success in business is no longer just about maximizing sales; nowadays, it's equally about building meaningful and lasting human-to-human connections.

To increase your prospects, then, you'll need to study what will work for your brand. And that means when it comes to creating and distributing your products, you'll have to *really* think carefully first.

Today's successful brands connect with their audience by tapping into a specific mindset or creating a unique persona. Every memorable brand has a distinct *personality*, something about it that emotionally connects with the audience.

Consider the MBC Group, for example, the biggest broadcasting conglomerate in the Middle East. For years now, their slogan has been 'We See Hope Everywhere'. This is their brand persona.

MBC creates an incredibly diverse range of content—drama series, flagship shows, chat shows, news documentaries, social messages, and so on—but 'We See Hope Everywhere' can be seen on every piece of content they create.

Far more than a mere slogan displayed on the company's headquarters, then, 'We See Hope Everywhere' is a sentiment that's deeply embedded within the MBC brand's DNA. Every show they produce embodies this ideal ...

Much like Damac, where I work right now. As a huge group, part of their largest business vertical is their real estate business, Damac Properties. Their slogan? 'Live The Luxury'.

This statement embodies DAMAC's unwavering commitment—one that is consistently communicated, represented, and delivered. Whether it's a AED 1 million home or a $20 million residence, DAMAC remains true to its core promise: *Live the Luxury*.

When Nike devised the slogan 'Just Do It', the phrase stuck, ultimately becoming its own empowering message. While every brand has its own persona, it's essential that they embed that persona within everything they do, making it part of their DNA. Within every communication piece, marketing campaign, and product on offer, that core promise must be a governing force.

To maintain credibility, every brand has to live by the promise they've made to their customers.

EXAMPLES OF THE HUMAN-CENTRIC APPROACH

To show the value of the humanized approach to branding, let's take a look at two compelling case studies, one from the Middle East and another with a global perspective.

First, let's journey to the Middle East, where the telecom giant Zain launched a Ramadan campaign titled 'Love Without Borders'. The campaign transcended traditional advertising by narrating stories of refugees and their struggles, thereby humanizing the brand and creating a deep emotional connection with its audience. The campaign increased Zain's brand visibility and significantly boosted customer loyalty and trust. It showcased the power of brands using their platform to address societal issues, leading to a profound impact. This initiative was not just about promoting telecom services; it also fostered a sense of unity and compassion, illustrating how brands can be pivotal in driving societal change.

On a global scale, Dove's 'Real Beauty' campaign stands out as a beacon of authentic storytelling. By questioning the conventional standards of beauty, Dove connected with women worldwide, promoting self-esteem and challenging beauty stereotypes. This campaign turned Dove from a mere soap manufacturer into a global advocate for women's confidence. The result was a staggering increase in sales and brand loyalty, proving that authenticity and social advocacy can drive both societal change and business success.

These case studies demonstrate that when brands prioritize authentic connections and address real-world issues, they achieve commercial success and contribute to positive societal change. The evidence is clear: Adopting a human-centric approach is not just beneficial; it's transformative for both the brand and its audience.

The Ultimate Shift

Since COVID, many brands have suddenly realized the importance of taking a human-centric sales approach.

The shift has taken place in three parts:

1. Well-Defined Communication

Creating an impactful marketing campaign requires crafting relevant messages. Most companies and brands now understand that the ability to create a human, emotional connection goes a long way; it's no longer about incessantly promoting a product, but about connecting with your audience instead. The only way to do this successfully, of course, is on a *human* level. Well-crafted messages that speak to the hearts and minds of consumers can elevate a brand to becoming a preferred choice.

2. Environmental, Social, and Governance Policy Strategy (ESG)

To add value, many brands are now examining their ESG in detail. In our environmentally conscious age, having a comprehensive and credible ESG has become a vital aspect of every brand's reputation. A sound ESG is no longer an accessory—it's a *necessity.* The stories brands tell should resonate emotionally with the audience, creating memorable experiences.

In order to work, an ESG has to be consistently applied across an entire corporation, including its associated entities. Credibly presenting such a policy to your board, investors, partners, and stakeholders requires impeccable accountability and compliance.

Yet with everyone talking about the importance of ESG policy, how do you implement ESG across your company's entire network? Further, how do you implement it within your products and make it central to your value proposition? With ESG now a necessity rather than a sideline, many companies are now playing catch-up. A crucial first step, however, is seeing the value of firmly embedding an ESG within the core business strategy and values.

3. Thought Leadership

In previous decades, thought leadership was not seen as an important aspect of business. Companies would hire someone to be their spokesperson, who would try their best to convey the company's vision to potential customers.

By contrast, thought leadership has now become a vital facet of all companies, giving credibility to the talent they have on board. Providing your executives or employees with credibility and exposure thus rubs off on your brand as well, conveying that the company has acquired top talent and managed to retain it. This speaks directly to customer trust and accountability. Because valuable employees arrived equipped with a wealth of knowledge and experience, the ability to reliably acquire such people portrays your company as one that's worth recognizing and investing in. In turn, this enhanced reputation makes it easier to acquire *more* talent (especially fresh graduates), with the improved public image boosting customer loyalty in the process.

This aspect of thought leadership aligns with the first two points above. When choosing between job offers, fresh graduates assess each company's value proposition, work–life balance, ESG policies, and overall working culture. So, given that your potential assets are no longer solely focused on a paycheck, but instead looking at all aspects of a company and brand, are you treating them in accordance with your ethics, values, and principles? Thought leadership also creates trust and accountability in the community, as well as valuable personal sub-brands within the organization.

Having the chance to work on a thought leadership strategy involves each employee with the wider company, helping create their personal brand. To build thought leadership, being active on LinkedIn and social media is highly recommended. Because inspiring positive change requires standing out with a clear purpose, genuine thought leadership encompasses far more than attending conferences, sitting on panels, and performing PR stunts. Instead, it's a long-term journey, involving building a relationship with an audience that genuinely trusts you.

FOCUSING ON PEOPLE
AND RELATIONSHIPS

An organization is primarily created by its people. That's why if I wanted to join an organization, either before or during the hiring process, I'd look at the leadership as well as the people they've hired. For example, having a trustworthy CEO who's willing to stake everything on their reputation says a lot about the organization. Similarly, who are the other people in the company, right across the board? What qualities do *they* have?

So, if a company's employees tend to be those with a certain type of background, experience, and profile, that says a lot about the organization. When you start thinking in this way, you'll start measuring the reputation of an organization by its people. If the employees *aren't* out there talking about the organization, about themselves, and about things that matter within the industry—and in the process, becoming industry leaders—how would the public know about the company's strengths? For that reason, you need those people to be out there facing the world. Using all the digital tools at your disposal to showcase your talent gives credibility to the organization. It also acts as a crisis management tool, because the people you take care of will serve as your brand ambassadors if any issues arise, speaking on behalf of the brand just as loyal customers would.

While these realizations occurred to many companies shortly before COVID hit, they *really* peaked afterwards. Purely sales-driven companies who didn't formerly believe in any of the three points above suddenly discovered the paramount importance of investing in individuals.

Culture and Communication

To succeed, it's important to invest in people's performance and internal development. Leaders need to regularly invest in ESG, as well as their employees' thought leadership and personal branding.

In addition, giving back to the community, accurately measuring impact, and developing a sustainability report are important tasks to complete annually.

In the process, you're aspiring to make your organization a Great Place to Work, making sure you thoroughly test it every year to gauge people's feeling towards their work environment (including work–life balance policies, salary increments, and bonuses). Achieving this certification will ensure that your commitment to fostering a positive and productive workplace is validated by an established and recognized standard.

To humanize their brand, organizations must have a strategy on how they hire and fire people, and of course how to retain staff. To foster an authentic audience connection, all internal and external communications must reinforce this central message.

In a world where C-suite executives are continually striving to distinguish themselves and their brands in a crowded and competitive marketplace, the challenge often lies in transcending traditional business strategies to forge a truly authentic and humanized brand identity.

My book addresses this critical need by offering a comprehensive methodology encapsulating Strategize, Act, and Impact—three pivotal steps designed to elevate personal and corporate branding to new heights. Through this approach, leaders are equipped to not only stay at the forefront of their industries, but also to create a lasting impact that resonates deeply with their audiences.

TAKEAWAYS

Brands must be infused with human-like qualities that foster genuine connections. This transformative shift from product-centric to human-centric branding, as well as the strategies for building a customer-centric culture, are rooted in empathy and feedback. The essence of authenticity is a core differentiator. The power of well-defined communication and storytelling to resound emotionally with audiences will heighten the impact of purpose-driven branding's alignment with greater societal causes.

The journey ahead is about translating these insights and strategies into actionable steps that will transform your brand into a living, breathing entity that your audience will feel deeply. Now, let's continue exploring how to make your brand not just seen but felt, remembered, and cherished.

In upcoming chapters, I'll reveal:

- How to build connections with the audience via purpose-driven branding that goes beyond traditional marketing
- How to build a customer-centric culture resembling the examples we've encountered, in which the internal matters as much as the external
- Crisis management where the internal culture matters as much as the external culture
- Connecting to the heartbeat of storytelling, thus building a long-term bond with the customer
- Engaging digital experiences, user-generated content, trust, and transparency
- The most effective way of personalizing brand experiences via authentic storytelling
- How to personalize brand experience by synergizing the personal and the organizational.

In doing so, I'll equip you, the reader, with enough knowledge to hit the ground running in our challenging corporate environment.

As a first step, let's get started on the most important aspect: your truth.

CHAPTER 3

THE POWER OF AUTHENTICITY

How to Build a Connection with Your Audience

In a world where everyone wears a mask, it's a privilege to see a soul. This quote by Amanda Richardson invites you to ponder the rarity and significance of authenticity in today's world. How often do you reveal your true self to others?

In any interaction, therefore, your message should be real. This fact is so simple that it often comes across as unrealistic and shocking. Building connections means that you don't have a hidden agenda. The connections aren't just transactional, but *transformative.*

Yet despite this crucial insight, marketers, brands, and corporations often strive to create a complicated story to share with their audience. In fact, by simply focusing on the truth about your brand—and in the process, explaining how what you're offering will help your audience—you'll make your message believable and worth communicating.

CUT THE CRAP AND GET REAL

Ask yourself: What's the real story?

It may surprise you that the answer's quite simple. When pondering this, you were probably tempted to come up with a complicated scenario, storyboard, or advertising campaign. Yet if you look deeply into an authentic customer-centric storytelling perspective, the solution's right there in front of you.

Meanwhile, you're hiring several agencies and paying through the nose to go big ... when to capture what's *real*, you just need to look at the customer.

Have you ever encountered a brand or a leader who seemed to speak directly to you, as if they understood exactly what you were going through? This connection wasn't accidental; it was forged by design, through the power of authenticity.

In today's Digital Age, where consumers are bombarded with countless messages and advertisements, the ability to stand out rests not only on the quality of what you have to offer, but even more so on the sincerity of your presentation. By embodying authenticity in your communication and actions, you answer the critical question: 'What's in it for me?' (WIIFM). In the process, you're showing your audience what they'll gain from engaging with you—and why they should care in the first place.

For example, during unusual weather events in April 2024, when everything had shut down, our company was in crisis mode, eagerly trying to reach out to customers, residents, and tenants. Then, after a few days had passed, we had a little bit of time to survey the impact of the disaster. This included the positive impact we'd created by being there for our clients, saving homes, attending to residents in distress, making sure the roads were clear, and confirming the safety and security processes were being handled properly by the authorities in partnership with our brand.

Today, our website communicates the story of that event (including positive testimonials on social media, which featured positive remarks on how well our team handled the crisis). Expressing appreciation for someone's efforts during difficult times can be as simple as a small caption on social media saying, 'Thank you, Damac, for handling this crisis so well.'

Sometimes it's so straightforward that people think, 'Oh no, it can't be that simple!' ... but it is.

So often in life, we look for complicated solutions to problems when the real answer's right in front of us. Creating connections means being there for others when genuinely needed, with no hidden agenda. It's all about authentically caring about somebody and empathizing with the situation they're in.

Of course, authenticity plays a big part when it comes to individual stories. If you're telling a story, you need to do so accurately. For that reason, instead of speaking inauthentically on someone else's behalf, you need to verify the story to ensure it's being conveyed respectfully and correctly.

As our fundamental exploration of authenticity, this chapter ventures deeply into how this concept impacts brands and corporations.

Communicating with Customers

These days, businesses rely on customers. Without customers, businesses cease to exist. It doesn't matter what you're selling. If you

THE POWER OF AUTHENTICITY

don't have a customer to buy it, your business is going nowhere. It's dead.

We need to reexamine the phrases 'Customers always come first' and 'The customer is always right'.

While I don't believe the customer is always right, I do believe the customer always comes first.

That's why post-COVID, we need to know how to communicate with our customers through clear and relevant messaging.

We can't speak to somebody in Singapore in exactly the same way as we speak to somebody in Dubai, for example. To make each of these people feel valued, you need to make the experience relevant to their particular context. If you do this skillfully, they'll think: 'Oh my God, Airbnb actually cares about me,' or 'Nike cares about me,' or 'Apple cares about me.'

It becomes a personalized message.

Look at any successful marketing or communication campaign that targets a certain segment of the community. One thing's clear: It's never 'one size fits all'.

A given campaign works only if the people creating it have a deep understanding of the customer's culture, background, language, traits, and habits. Armed with this information, you can work out how to best communicate with that customer. Therefore, it's never 'one size fits all', because you can't have a simple overarching message whose impact is equal across the globe.

After all, if you don't know the customer, how are you ever going to personalize your message?

Another important layer of messaging is the emotions. You need to appeal to people's emotions, which will humanize the narrative and facilitate communication.

For this reason, the messaging is different when you're addressing a family compared to a single person. Understanding the audience is vital to communicating in a personalized manner.

Due to this emphasis on personal qualities, mass production is no longer appealing. People are spoilt for choice, only desiring what's unique to them. Because every person wants to feel special, they'll only respond to stories which touch their heart while connecting with their needs. Yet at the same time, you have to be mindful of the practicalities of business. This form of communication makes both emotional and financial sense, because the heart and mind work hand in hand.

Over time, this awareness of each customer's individuality builds up their loyalty, establishing an enduring bridge of trust.

This mode of connection is all around us. For example, you'll hear some people say, 'Oh, no, I only buy Nike. I don't buy a certain brand.' Or other people say, 'I'm a very Nike person.'

Even with mobile phones—Apple versus Samsung—for the customer, it's the way the services or features speak to them. We're all affiliated with certain brands, with our bond depending on how we've connected with them throughout our lives, combined with how they communicate with us as individuals.

AUTHENTICITY:
THE ESSENCE OF CONNECTION

At the heart of every meaningful human interaction lies authenticity. It's the quality that makes conversations genuine, relationships deep, and experiences memorable. When brands apply this quality, they're able to create connections that are transformative.

Authenticity, in the context of branding, is about staying true to one's core values and identity. It's about conveying a consistent message that aligns with the genuine intentions of the brand. This level of alignment establishes a bridge of trust between the brand and its audience, creating a sense of familiarity, relatability, and reliability.

Consider Airbnb's journey. By tapping into the innate human desire for connection and adventure, Airbnb reframed travel from a transactional experience to a human one. The platform became more than just a means to find accommodation; it transformed into a conduit for authentic cultural experiences. By aligning their messaging with this relatable human desire, Airbnb created an emotional connection that transcended traditional marketing tactics.

Case Study: Airbnb—Crafting Connections Through Experience

Airbnb's 'Belong Anywhere' campaign exemplifies the power of authenticity in branding. Instead of focusing solely on the accommodation itself, Airbnb positioned their platform as a way for travelers to experience destinations like locals. The brand's messaging resonated with the innate human desire for connection and belonging. By focusing on the authentic experiences users could have through their platform, Airbnb built a loyal and engaged community.

Steps to Connect with an Authentic Message

What steps can somebody follow to understand how to develop credibility by building up that kind of authenticity and connection?

First, you need to know what your brand stands for. What are you selling, and why? How, when, and where are you selling it? Why does your company exist? How are you planning to communicate with your audience?

The answer's as simple as knowing your brand's 'why'. The entire brand revolves around the 'why'. If you're a developer, you're selling dream homes. If you're a sports brand, you're creating dreams and future athletes. If you're selling cosmetics, you're promoting genuine beauty or flawless skin.

If you're into clothing, for example, you're catering to all sizes and shapes because you believe in diversity. All successful brands in the past decade, including Dove, Real Beauty, and H&M, have a retail line for larger women. Most high-visibility brands now embody a real message. If you look at P&G and their campaign with Ariel, their message—'Share the Load'—was particularly resonant in India.

The 'Share the Load' campaign is a well-known advertising initiative originally launched by the detergent brand Ariel, part of P&G. This campaign started in India in 2015 and focused on addressing the issue of gender inequality in household chores, specifically laundry, which is often considered a woman's responsibility. Every communication needs to have a human connection, because you're selling the 'why'. Some of the elements of this campaign are:

a. Problem Statement: The campaign highlighted the unequal distribution of household chores, questioning why laundry and other domestic tasks are often expected to be done by women. It aimed to challenge deep-rooted stereotypes around gender roles.

b. Emotional Storytelling: The campaign used emotionally charged advertisements that portrayed real-life scenarios, such as fathers apologizing to their daughters for not setting a better example in sharing household responsibilities, and husbands realizing their own role in perpetuating inequality.

c. Call to Action: The core message was simple but powerful— Encourage everyone, especially men, to take a step forward and share the responsibility of laundry and other household chores. The hashtag #ShareTheLoad became a rallying point for social media discussions.

d. Impact: The campaign received widespread recognition for sparking conversations about gender equality at home. It not only boosted Ariel's brand image but also won several awards, including Cannes Lions and Effie Awards, for its innovative approach to social issues through marketing.

e. Extensions: Due to its success, the campaign was extended into multiple phases over the years, each time evolving to address new insights, including how unequal chores impacted children's perspectives on gender roles.

This campaign is often cited as a prime example of how brands can leverage purpose-driven marketing to address social issues, create impactful narratives, and connect deeply with audiences beyond the product. This 'why' creates brand affiliation, loyalty, credibility, and trust. So, if increasing your market share is your 'why', how exactly are you going to do that? You'll get people on board through connecting with their heart and mind. You need to create a story where people say, 'I'm *definitely* buying Pampers'. Even in times of humanitarian crisis, brand affiliation enables companies to stand out. For example, when Procter & Gamble partnered with UNICEF about a decade ago, they offered one pack of nappies with every vaccine administered to a child in Africa.

In fact, to add to this brand story, when I realized my son was allergic to Pampers, I had to switch to another brand. One day, walking through the diaper aisle at the supermarket, I looked at Pampers and saw their affiliation with UNICEF. I thought, 'Hmm, maybe my son's no longer allergic. Maybe I'll give these a try.' When I looked at the box, I immediately thought: 'Wow, if I pick this up, I'll actually have done something good with my money by contributing to children's welfare without making an extra effort.' So, I bought the package.

These associations make potential customers feel good by making them feel connected with a brand they perceive as responsible. With the right audience, stories like these can really hit the mark.

Another reason to foster authenticity is ESG. Post-COVID, most celebrities, public figures, leaders, and companies are starting to understand that social responsibility plays a huge role when it comes to branding.

When considering a product, people will now look for a responsible humanitarian brand that places people and the planet above profit. If you're claiming to help save the Earth, having sustainable, environmentally friendly initiatives is crucial. Here, the three Ps come together—profit, planet, and people (PPP, the 'triple bottom line'). This also means that when you create profits, you're creating stronger economies at the same time. If you're looking after your people, you're adding value to your country. And if you're looking after your planet, you're contributing to Earth's wellbeing.

In response, most companies, both globally and regionally, have started scrutinizing their PPP and ESG policies for guidance on how to implement environmental, social, and governance policies and strategies in line with their DNA (instead of just lip-synching).

The Chief Communications Officer (CCO) is an integral part of this process, ensuring everybody's connected and the right message reaches the public. In doing so, they have to work very closely with the Chief Marketing Officer. These two people are critical to any organization, responsible for keeping these values embedded within every strategy and business vertical. A CCO is the spokesperson who tirelessly talks about these values across the board, whether internally or externally, on multiple channels (social media, TV, radio, podcast, newspaper articles, and so on). Everybody needs to get on board, and the core message needs to be integrated within the company's DNA.

In short, everybody needs to walk the talk.

TAKEAWAYS

Brands are now taking a 360-degree approach. It's no longer only CSR (corporate social responsibility), or only marketing, or only communication, or only advertising. Instead, it refers to everybody working together towards the ultimate goal, which is creating and maintaining a responsible brand. Now, a responsible brand doesn't mean that we're not profitable. Instead, a responsible brand means that we make money while treating our people, our communities, and the planet with respect. This means keeping it real, placing the human factor at the center of it all.

To do this, companies must do the following:

- Decide on three or four core values that serve as their Bible when it comes to branding.
- Consolidate the entire communication and marketing strategy and direction.
- Run internal awareness sessions and campaigns to get everybody on board with the new brand values.
- Explain why this is of value to everybody, including the wider business. (Why is this going to make any difference? Why do we need you to implement it? How is this going to work, and what do we need from you?)
- Clearly elucidate the why, the how, the what, and the when.
- Promote internal champions to get everybody excited about, and on board with, the new direction. (To do this, you need to communicate it across the board. It shouldn't only be coming from the Chief Executive—if it does, it will die out as it trickles down.)
- Ensure accountability across every single department, which will enable changes to be consistently implemented.
- Simply demonstrate *how* these changes will be implemented across the board.
- Last but not least, somebody needs to champion this. And that person is the company's Chief Communications Officer.

Creating a corporate video is a great awareness tool to send out and keep on your platforms. This makes sure everybody is aware of your brand values and knows what you stand for, both as a company and as individuals.

We're not just talking about the bottom line, either—we're talking profit and purpose *together*. The P and the P work hand in hand, because doing good makes good business sense in our modern world. When you give back to the community, the community will automatically give back to you, a truth which leads us to the purpose behind the brand.

CHAPTER 4

PURPOSE-DRIVEN BRANDING

Beyond Traditional Marketing

Traditional marketing is no longer working in the Digital Age. You remember those Hallmark moments from an era when people actually mailed greeting cards to each other?

It's time to bring them back.

Hallmark is like the OG creator of emotional content before TikTok made it cool. The phrase 'OG creator' is a shorthand way of saying 'original creator.' By referring to Hallmark as the 'OG creator of emotional content,' it means that they were pioneering and innovating in this space well before other platforms.

Hallmark is best known for those greeting cards, movies, and holiday specials that capture 'all the feels'—from celebrating birthdays to those cheesy but comforting Christmas movies. Think of Hallmark as the brand that makes life's small and big moments feel special, using words and stories to connect people, often in a very heartfelt (and sometimes super-sugary) way.

Hallmark products are all about spreading joy, kindness, and a sense of nostalgia. It's that cozy vibe you get from handwritten notes, feelgood movies, and thoughtful gifts—things that hit differently in a world that's mostly digital. Whether it's a cute card for your bestie or a rom-com you binge-watch with your family, Hallmark is all about keeping the art of personal connection alive.

The key is to highlight Hallmark's nostalgic value, the personal touch it brings in an increasingly digital era, and its enduring appeal through its movies and cards, which still resonate as ways to express emotions authentically.

Traditional marketing techniques—in other words, just talking about the product and how it's a good investment, or trying to sell it for profit's sake alone without touching on the emotional side—simply don't work anymore.

So, it's time to look at the brand's overall goal, including how it affects the communities around it and why you're selling this product to begin with. To put it bluntly, why are you in this particular industry? To answer this convincingly, you'll need to discover a heartfelt method of content creation, namely videos and stories. Any genuinely effective brand will forge this intense connection between heart and head, so that customers are compelled to talk about your company without being prompted. Success is no longer about relentlessly talking up a brand or product; instead, it's now about enticing other people to do the talking on your behalf.

A brand that's capable of harnessing these human connections is *genuinely* purpose-driven.

DEFINING PURPOSE-DRIVEN BRANDING

Purpose-driven branding isn't about sporadic acts of charity or token efforts; it's about embedding a brand's core values, mission, and impact into every facet of its existence. The brand's purpose becomes a guiding light that directs its strategies, products, marketing, and even organizational culture.

As we navigate through the Digital Age, it's becoming increasingly clear that the old marketing playbook is no longer as effective. Consumers are seeking more from the brands they support than just the goods or services they purchase; they're looking for a reflection of their own values and beliefs in the companies they choose to engage with. This shift has given rise to the importance of purpose-driven branding—a strategy that focuses on highlighting a brand's mission, vision, and values to create a lasting impact and foster a strong, loyal community.

In this chapter, we'll look into the nuances of building a brand that resonates with its audience on a deeper level. By the end, you'll have gained a clear understanding of how to articulate your brand's unique values, mission, and vision in a way that differentiates you from the competition and builds a meaningful connection with your customers. You'll learn the art of evaluating and refining your brand's personality and tone of voice to ensure consistency across all touchpoints, making it more relatable and accessible.

Furthermore, this chapter will guide you through the process of conducting comprehensive brand audits. This crucial step helps identify potential areas for growth and alignment, ensuring that every aspect of your brand strategy is cohesive and purpose-driven. By focusing on these key elements, you'll be equipped to craft a branding strategy that will stand the test of time, positively influencing your target audience and society at large.

Walking the Talk

Why should someone care about your brand? What sets you apart in a sea of competitors? It's not just about the features of your product or the services you offer; it's about the impact you're making. Whether your mission is to empower individuals, advance sustainability, or bring joy through innovation, your purpose is what guides your brand.

Doing this requires creating a brand or message that positively impacts our world. Whether this is a chewing gum, a detergent, a service, or even a spacecraft, the way you communicate its strengths makes a huge difference.

If it's done right, building a human-centric story around the product will create a profound connection with the audience while conveying a compelling sense of purpose. For example, you could say that with every 10,000 packets of chewing gum sold, we're going to put someone through college or give them a scholarship.

In this vein, consider the unforgettable story told by the shoe brand Toms. If you buy one pair, Toms donate a second pair to less privileged families in Africa and Asia—a level of social commitment that rapidly creates positive associations. Customers feel heartened that not only are Toms using eco-friendly material to create their shoes, but they're also considering how to create a positive impact for children worldwide. Now *that's* a purpose-driven brand.

That's a brand which looks beyond their profit and loss (P&L) statement. That's a brand which, while still considering profit, is at the same time adding value and positively impacting humanity. In reality, these are the brands that last the longest. When it comes to a workplace crisis, a natural disaster, or an economic or financial crisis, you not only retain your people, but your customers as well. In these circumstances, these people will feel as if they belong to a brand that's actually responsible and purposeful. At the same time, they'll appreciate how much you've already given to the community, so will stand by you no matter what. That's how you create champions on the ground who are comfortable spontaneously speaking up on your behalf. *That's a purpose-driven brand.*

While products and services fulfill functional needs, a brand's purpose fulfills emotional and aspirational ones. The concept of purpose answers the question: 'Why does the brand exist beyond making profit?' Purpose taps into the deeper yearnings of individuals, resonating with their deeply held values and desires.

The Power of Connectivity and Purpose

If there's a crisis situation, are you going to boycott the brand that stands for a social purpose or humanitarian cause? Or are you going to boycott the one that only cares about profit, with no health-related or human-centric values involved in their business? The answer is obvious.

During any crisis, whether it's political, economic, or social, people tend to look at the brands that have contributed to society, rather than the ones that only care about the bottom line. They'll boycott the profit-obsessed brands, standing by those that have actually given back to society in the past, as well as to the communities that actually buy their product.

It could be that the purpose-driven brand has created jobs for the low-income communities. They may have built schools or healthcare centers, provided clean water to remote areas and villages, mended roads, and created valuable infrastructure. Help and purpose come in different shapes and sizes, and purpose is not one-size-fits-all. It depends on how large or small your enterprise is. But the fact is, whether you're an SME or a large conglomerate, you can still make the difference. It depends on how you start.

Based in the Middle East and North Africa (MENA) region, Souk El Hima (Market of the Protected Area) offers a compelling example of purpose-driven branding (https://www.spnl.org/souk-el-hima-lebanon/). This initiative supports conservation efforts while empowering local communities by promoting sustainable products derived from Hima areas (protected zones managed by traditional communities). By linking environmental conservation with economic development, Souk El Hima has preserved local wildlife and habitats while improving livelihoods, showcasing the power of purpose in driving both brand success and societal change.

MY PURPOSE-DRIVEN JOURNEY

On a personal note, integrating purpose into my brand was a journey of transformation. It began with identifying a gap in the market for products that served a practical purpose while promoting a cause. By aligning my brand with efforts to improve education in underprivileged communities, we offered value to our customers and contributed to a cause greater than ourselves. This shift wasn't without its challenges, requiring a reevaluation of our supply chain, marketing strategies, and even our internal culture. However, the rewards have been immeasurable, with increased customer loyalty, employee satisfaction, and a stronger brand presence in the market.

Our efforts culminated in a partnership with local schools, where a portion of every sale went towards improving educational facilities and resources. This initiative bolstered our brand's image and engaged our customers in our mission, creating a community of advocates for education. The journey taught me the undeniable power of a purpose-driven brand to make a real difference in the world, transcending traditional business objectives to leave a lasting impact on society.

Integrating the ethos of purpose-driven branding into a brand's strategy can significantly elevate its impact on and connection with its audience. Adding another dimension to this narrative is the examination of Patagonia, a globally recognized brand that exemplifies the power of purpose in business.

Patagonia: A Living Manifestation of Purpose

Patagonia, an outdoor clothing company which transformed itself into an environmental activist brand, stands as an embodiment of purpose-driven branding. Patagonia's purpose is evident in its commitment to protecting the planet. From donating a significant portion of profits to environmental causes to launching campaigns advocating for conservation, Patagonia's purpose has become the heart and soul of the brand.

Begin with the Betterment of Humanity in Mind: MBC Hope

MBC is the leading broadcasting conglomerate in the MENA region, with the MBC Hope brand recognizing the power of human stories to connect with audiences. In 'Voices of Hope', we shared real stories of individuals whose lives were transformed through our community initiatives. By highlighting personal journeys, we showcased how doing good made good business sense, fostering a deep emotional connection with our audience. The campaign not only increased brand loyalty but also positioned MBC Hope as a compassionate and impactful organization in the region.

As the Head of Corporate Social Responsibility at MBC Group, I was keen to grow my division and effect long-term impact in the region. My goal aimed to empower Arab youth and leverage the company's resources and capabilities to establish MBC Group as a leader in CSR. The case study at https://hbsp.harvard.edu/product/SCM103-PDF-ENG describes the strategies and programs that MBC Al Amal, the CSR arm of MBC Group, implemented in order to achieve this goal, as well as potential areas of improvement (https://www.thecasecentre.org/products/view?id=173505).

In any branding exercise, it's important to determine your mission and vision. What do you stand for as a company? For example, if you're a food and beverage brand producing soft drinks, you consume a lot of water to make those drinks. Consequently, you need to find a way to give back a lot of that water. So, that's when you take a stand to ensure clean water for everyone. To compensate for the damage you're doing to the communities and the environment, you create wells and improve access to clean water, electricity, and so on.

If you're in oil and gas, you're already polluting the oceans and the sea. So, stand for something that aligns with your business, like marine biology research. Stand for clean oceans, or for the preservation of certain islands that are in the process of being submerged.

Every business needs to adopt a purpose, policy, or social cause that aligns with the damage they're creating in the world, I'm sorry to say, even if you're *not* creating damage, and you're just a business that wants to give back, it's important to align these efforts with your brand identity. You can't just be looking into eradicating cancer because it's sexy. Instead, this objective must align with your brand values, clearly linked to the purpose of your entire business. Importantly, this objective needs to be sustainable.

I wouldn't like to see brands sending out donations without knowing either where they're going or how they're being measured. Writing those big checks and snapping pictures in front of them is no longer appealing; no one's doing that anymore.

MEASURE THE IMPACT

If you're going to create a purpose-driven brand that's capable of great things, you'll need to measure it accurately. Create an in-house volunteer program to make sure your people are thoroughly integrated with the brand's purpose. It's not only about funding outside organizations—you're also creating a people-first environment internally, capable of getting people engaged by making them feel as if they're adding value to your brand's overall purpose.

Purpose-driven brands aren't confined to the status quo; they become trailblazers in their industries. Purpose sparks innovation by challenging traditional norms and prompting creative solutions that align with the brand's mission. It's about finding innovative ways to address societal challenges and contribute positively to the world.

Shaping the Narrative

Purpose transforms a brand's narrative from a mere marketing spiel into a compelling story that captures hearts and minds.

Yet this purpose-driven strategy won't work if the brand cynically adopts it as a PR stunt for marketing purposes. If it's not authentic, it will die out. It's going to actually harm, rather than help, the brand's reputation. The purpose behind a brand is a long-term, sustainable, and heartfelt strategy, not a short-term marketing ploy. The company executives have to believe in their purpose, with the messaging flowing from top to bottom—because if the leaders themselves don't believe in their own brand's purpose, it'll never work. They *really* need to feel this is important for everyone to adopt. When your aims align with your business, you can improve your return on investment (ROI).

How are you measuring this, though? It could be reputational, or it could be in terms of sales figures, customer loyalty, or attracting more investment. Are the shareholders happy and satisfied? You might be interested in market share, or how the voices across the various digital platforms are affecting your reputation.

Every brand has differing KPIs, along with different ways of measuring these as well as their ROIs. What *doesn't* change, though, is accountability. KPIs have to be clear, as do the methods used to measure your ROIs. Measuring must be systematic, so you can reliably gauge how your brand is reaching its target values. You can't just say, 'Oh yeah, we're helping kids in Africa.' Show me how many kids you've actually helped, then communicate these numbers to the outside world. For a brand, knowing *how* you've helped a cause gives the company accountability and credibility.

The 'What' and 'How' of a Purpose-Driven Brand

1. Learn How to Hook Through Purpose

a. Understand Your Unique Value Proposition (USP): Dig deep to identify what makes your brand uniquely positioned to address the needs or desires of your audience. This isn't just about what you sell, but the unique way you solve a problem or enhance others' lives.

b. Simplify Your Message: Once you've homed in on your purpose, distill it into a simple, compelling message that can be communicated in a matter of seconds. This clarity ensures that your audience immediately understands the value you offer.

c. Use Visuals and Stories: People are naturally drawn to stories and images that evoke emotion. Use powerful visuals and storytelling to encapsulate your purpose, making it both memorable and shareable.

2. Identify Your Identity, Then Your Purpose

a. Define What You Stand For: Beyond your products or services, what are the core principles and values that define your brand? These should be non-negotiable elements that inform all your decisions.

b. Align Your Offerings with Your Purpose: Every product, service, and piece of content should clearly align with your brand's identity and purpose. This alignment ensures coherence and strengthens your brand's message.

c. Communicate Authentically: Authenticity can't be faked. Ensure that your communication is genuine and reflects the true spirit of your brand. Authenticity fosters trust and loyalty among your audience.

3. Innovation Through Purpose

a. Foster a Culture of Innovation: Encourage a culture within your organization that sees innovation as a means to further your purpose. This includes being open to new ideas, taking calculated risks, and always looking for better ways to serve your mission.

b. Link Innovations to Your Brand Story: Every innovation should tell a part of your brand's story, emphasizing how it contributes to the broader mission. This connection makes your innovations more meaningful to your audience.

c. Celebrate Failures and Successes: Innovation involves risks, and not all initiatives will succeed. Celebrate both the failures and the successes as part of your journey, learning from each to continuously improve.

4. Purpose is the Storyline

a. Embed Purpose in Your Brand DNA: Your brand's purpose should be so deeply ingrained in its DNA that every aspect of the business reflects it. This includes your internal culture, how you interact with customers, and how you contribute to the community.

b. Create a Community Around Your Purpose: Build a community of like-minded individuals who share your brand's values and mission. This creates a powerful network effect, amplifying your message and impact.

c. Leverage Feedback Loops: Use feedback from your community to refine and evolve your purpose-driven strategy. This iterative process ensures that your brand remains relevant and aligned with your audience's values and needs.

Step-by-Step Brand Example

Consider a hypothetical tech startup, GreenTech Innovations, that's dedicated to creating sustainable technology solutions. Their journey might look something like this:

1. Purpose Identification: GreenTech Innovations is focused on reducing the carbon footprint of the tech industry through renewable energy–powered devices.

2. Message Simplification: The company's slogan becomes 'Powering the Future, Sustainably.'

3. Product Alignment: Every product launched by GreenTech Innovations is energy-efficient and uses recycled materials, embodying the company's commitment to sustainability.

4. Innovative Solutions: They introduce a solar-powered smartphone, disrupting the market with a product that appeals to environmentally conscious consumers.

5. Community Engagement: GreenTech Innovations hosts an annual 'GreenTech Challenge'. By encouraging innovators to propose new eco-friendly tech solutions, they foster a community of sustainability advocates.

Get Started

To transition from insights gleaned to impactful actions, it's essential to undertake a series of deliberate steps. These steps will refine your brand's identity and market position, deepening its connection with your audience. Here's a comprehensive roadmap for your next actions:

1. Take a Deep Dive Into Your Personal and Brand Purpose: Reflect deeply on what motivates you and the broader impact you envision for your brand. This dual discovery process is crucial. Begin by asking yourself:

'What am I passionate about?'

'How does this passion align with my brand?'

Then, explore how your brand can serve as a vehicle for this purpose, asking:

'What unique role can my brand play in making a difference?'

This foundational step is about aligning your personal values with your brand's mission, ensuring they're in harmony and driving towards a common goal.

2. Articulate and Refine What Your Brand Stands For: Clarify your brand's core values and mission statement. This involves more than just listing desirable qualities; it requires a deeper understanding of the impact you wish to have and the legacy you aim to create. Consider holding workshops with your team to collectively identify these values and ensure everyone is aligned with the brand's purpose.

3. Thoroughly Evaluate Your Brand's Personality and Tone: Assess whether your brand's voice is authentic and whether it resonates

with your target demographic. Analyze your brand's current communication across various channels—social media, your website, email newsletters, and any other customer touchpoints. Ask, 'Do these communications reflect our values and purpose?' and 'How do our customers perceive and react to our brand's personality?'. This step is about consistency and authenticity in how your brand presents itself and interacts with its audience.

4. Conduct Comprehensive Brand Audits: Conducting a brand audit is a multifaceted process that involves examining your brand's market presence, customer perceptions, and internal alignment with your purpose and values. This should be a regular part of your strategy to identify not just areas for improvement but also opportunities for innovation and deeper engagement. Look at customer feedback, analyze performance data, and stay attuned to shifts in the market that might affect your brand's relevance and impact.

5. Create a Purpose-Driven Action Plan: Based on the insights from your brand audits and evaluations, develop a strategic plan that outlines specific, actionable steps to enhance your brand's alignment with its purpose. This plan should include goals for storytelling, community engagement, product development, and any other areas relevant to your brand's mission. Each goal should have clear metrics for success, ensuring that your brand's purpose is not just aspirational, but actively guiding your business decisions and growth.

6. Engage Your Audience in Your Purpose: Look for creative and impactful ways to involve your customers and the wider community

in your brand's purpose. This could mean organizing community events, launching social impact initiatives, or creating content that educates and inspires action. The goal is to transform your audience from passive consumers into active participants in your brand's mission.

As you move forward, remember that the journey of integrating purpose into your brand is ongoing and ever-evolving. It demands continuous reflection, learning, and adaptation.

TAKEAWAYS

Purpose-driven branding is more than a marketing strategy; it's also focused on the good of the people. Loyal customers empower brands to do better, signaling a cultural shift within the brand and its interactions with the world. Brands like Patagonia demonstrate that when purpose becomes a brand's driving force, it transforms businesses into agents of positive change. As readers, what's the potential of your brand not just to sell products, but to inspire and elevate communities, society, and even the world at large?

Now, we'll delve into an important factor to propel your business forward. Organizations that work towards building these purposeful brands have a dedicated team of people who are all working towards a common goal. Let's see how they do it.

CHAPTER 5

BUILDING A CUSTOMER-CENTRIC BRAND

Aligning Internal and External Culture

How can we expect to treat our customers well if we don't first take care of our people internally?

This question relates to a fundamental truth in business: The treatment of employees within an organization directly affects the quality of customer service and overall customer experience. The internal and external cultures of an organization are deeply interconnected, highlighting the importance of nurturing a harmonious, customer-centric environment at all levels.

By the end of this chapter, you'll have the knowledge and tools necessary to cultivate a workplace environment that prioritizes and reflects the values and expectations of your customers, as well as strategies for fostering empathy and active listening within your organization. These are crucial skills that empower employees to understand and anticipate customer needs, leading to more meaningful interactions and stronger relationships. You'll discover practical ways to embed these principles into your daily operations from the leadership level down, creating a ripple effect that enhances every touchpoint with your brand.

Ensuring that the customer remains loyal to the brand leads us to building a customer-centric culture. Now, customer-centric culture means aligning the internal culture with the external. It's about creating authenticity with a brand that clearly reflects the company's purpose. This is coupled with the customer-centricity of our modern world in the Digital Age. Having customers is one thing, but maintaining their loyalty and trust requires another level of connection.

This starts with being honest about your brand. You can't sell something, then fail to deliver on what you're promising. So if you're promising that your shampoo will reduce dandruff, you need to deliver on that promise. If you're promising great quality in an apartment, you need to deliver on that. And on top of all this, if you made a mistake but failed to address it, you need to admit that you've done so, then either recall the product or (if it's something that can't be recalled) apologize and rectify the situation. Then, you share the measurements on how you're going to improve your product deliverables in the future.

IT ALL STARTS FROM HOME

Number one is transparency and honesty. Number two is delivering on promises. And number three is actually taking care of your people.

Nurturing a positive internal culture is essential for any organization aiming to excel in customer service, and by extension brand reputation. How can we expect to promise excellent customer service when we're treating our *own* people like garbage?

So, explore how you treat your people first, because they're your best brand ambassadors. If they're happy and they feel looked after, appreciated, and valued, they'll be the ones out there talking up your company, your brand, and your personal leadership qualities.

Start on home ground—your organization. Make sure there's a great culture internally, which will automatically have a knock-on effect. By talking positively about the brand they work for, employees become great ambassadors.

If you share an article on LinkedIn or Instagram explaining how great your customer service and culture is, readers will generally agree. They *won't* say, 'Oh no, you're such liars.' They'll tend to agree, and even boast about being associated with your company.

On the other hand, many companies who claim to have a great culture actually don't, because they lack inclusive cultures or diverse processes and procedures. They don't treat people equally or enforce equal pay policies, failing to create a balance between wellness and working life or care about each individual's needs. To them, each human is just a cog in a machine that keeps the organization running.

Post-COVID, everybody's looking at that great employer with the attitude of 'What's in it for me? Why should I work for *you*?'. It's not the other way around anymore. If an organization's going to acquire top talent, especially fresh graduates, they need to be honest about their internal culture.

Building an internal culture that encourages happiness and fulfilment is not merely an internal HR initiative; it's a strategic business move. Happy employees lead to happy customers, which, in turn, lead to a stronger, more resilient brand.

Organizations can cultivate such an environment, ensuring that the values they project externally to customers are lived and breathed internally by every member of the team. The journey towards aligning internal culture with the external brand promise is both challenging and rewarding.

Employee Storytelling Campaigns: We Are Damac

At the company I work for, Damac, we launched an internal campaign titled 'We Are Damac' to humanize our brand and boost employee engagement. This initiative featured stories of employees from different departments, highlighting their contributions and personal growth within the company. These stories were shared through internal newsletters, social media, and company events. By celebrating our employees, we fostered a sense of pride and loyalty, which translated into improved customer engagement and a positive brand image externally.

Creating the Culture

Respect is a central element. Besides that, trust, accountability, responsibility, and communication are all crucial to communicating a sense of appreciation, acknowledgement, and reward. A proper performance management system can actually address weaknesses while acknowledging strengths, offering support for talent and development. Capacity-building is an integral part of your offering, so investing in your people and leadership with purpose is key. Choose your organization's leaders wisely, ensuring they're role models when it comes to leadership. While leadership style differs from one person to another, overall there has to be an innate sense of respect across the board. You can't have disrespectful people working for you, because they'll eventually push others away.

Employees quit their *bosses*, not their jobs. For this reason, looking at how the top managers are actually managing, leading, and treating their people is very important. Accountability means making sure there's a safe haven for all employees to inform a responsible entity whenever they're facing difficulties (be it HR or another department); this will reassure them that they have a safe place to voice their concerns.

Creating clear policies and processes for people internally means creating an environment that's mentally and physically healthy for employees' wellbeing. Working from home is much more common nowadays than it previously was, making possible increased time with family. Respecting this need for all employees fosters an invaluable sense of belonging to the company.

This culture is not just about frontline customer service; it covers every part of the organization, from the internal structure to how employees embody the brand's values in their day-to-day activities. Here are the steps necessary to cultivate an environment that ensures both employees and customers feel valued and understood.

Leaders Who Value People

For this to work, the organization needs to create an internal culture which accurately reflects the external customer-centric environment. From there, everything builds. People view the company from a perspective that's not just reputational, but also in terms of how they support the internal employees and staff. Considering this fact leads to strategies for fostering empathy. If you don't have empathetic leaders, you'll risk losing your best people.

While nurturing active listening and collaboration among employees is great, a company's potential can be further boosted by discouraging office politics and eradicating glass ceilings for anyone—women, different ethnicities, and any other minority groups that may be marginalized. Give people a chance to grow based on their potential, skills, and talents.

The Embodiment of a Culture

Building a customer-centric culture within an organization is a transformative process that demands an intentional and strategic approach. This culture covers frontline customer service and every part of the organization, from the internal structure to how employees embody the brand's values in their day-to-day activities. Here are the steps necessary to cultivate an environment that ensures both employees and customers feel valued and understood.

1. Creating Internal Structure

The foundation of a customer-centric culture is a well-defined internal structure that supports and encourages customer-focused behaviors. This structure includes organizational hierarchies, workflows, and communication systems designed to streamline processes and enhance the quality of service provided to customers.

How to Do It:

- Optimize Organizational Design: Reassess and, if necessary, reorganize your company's structure to ensure it supports direct and efficient communication and decision-making processes with the customer's needs in mind.
- Empower Teams: Enable teams by giving them the autonomy to make customer-centric decisions. This empowerment can lead to innovative solutions that directly enhance customer satisfaction.
- Foster Interdepartmental Collaboration: Break down silos within the organization to ensure all departments work towards a unified goal of customer satisfaction. Encourage regular interdepartmental meetings to share insights and strategies.

2. Employee Branding Initiatives

Employees are the most authentic brand ambassadors. Their belief in and commitment to the brand's mission can significantly influence its perception in the market. Employee branding initiatives aim to instill a deep understanding and appreciation of the brand's values and goals among all staff members.

How to Do It:

- Integrate Brand Values into Daily Operations: Make brand values a part of everyday conversations and decisions. This continuous exposure helps employees internalize these values.

- Create Brand Champions: Identify and train key employees to act as brand champions within the organization. They can lead by example and motivate others to follow suit.
- Leverage Internal Marketing: Use internal marketing strategies to consistently communicate the brand's mission, upcoming campaigns, and customer success stories to all employees.

3. Fostering Positive Internal Culture on Various Levels

A positive internal culture is characterized by mutual respect, open communication, and a shared commitment to excellence. Cultivating such a culture requires deliberate actions that encourage these qualities across all levels of the organization.

How to Do It:

- Implement Regular Training and Development Programs: Continuous learning opportunities can motivate employees and help them feel valued. Tailor these programs to not only develop skills but also reinforce the company's commitment to customer-centricity.
- Cultivate a Feedback-Rich Environment: Encourage and facilitate regular feedback among employees and between employees and management. This should include recognition of customer-centric actions and constructive discussions on areas of improvement.
- Celebrate Successes: Recognize and celebrate achievements that reflect the organization's customer-centric values. This could range from small acts of going above and beyond for a customer to major project completions.

4. Enhancing the Employee Journey: Hiring to Exiting

The employee experience, from recruitment to departure, should reflect and reinforce the organization's customer-centric values. Each stage of the employee lifecycle offers an opportunity to embed these values deeper into the company culture.

How to Do It:

- Recruit with a Customer-Centric Lens: During recruitment, look for candidates who not only have the required skill set but also demonstrate a natural inclination towards empathy and customer service.
- Purpose-Driven Onboarding: Use the onboarding process to immerse new hires in the company's customer-centric culture, showing them how their role contributes to the broader mission.
- Conduct Insightful Exit Interviews: Leverage exit interviews as a tool to gain honest feedback on the organization's culture and practices. This feedback can be invaluable in making improvements.

5. 360-Degree Culture

A 360-degree culture means that the organization's customer-centric values are evident in every interaction, both internal and external. Achieving this level of consistency requires a holistic approach to embedding these values into the organization's DNA.

How to Do It:

- Align Leadership and Management: Ensure that leaders and managers across the organization embody customer-centric values in their leadership style. They should actively promote these values through their actions and decisions.
- Build a Supportive Environment: Create an environment where employees feel supported in their efforts to prioritize the customer. This includes providing the necessary tools, resources, and authority to resolve customer issues effectively.
- Monitor and Adjust: Use regular assessments of the company culture and customer feedback to identify areas for improvement. Be prepared to make adjustments to policies, procedures, and practices to better align with customer-centric goals.

In implementing these strategies, remember that building a customer-centric culture is a dynamic process that evolves with your organization and its customers.

To further illustrate the transformative impact of a customer-centric culture within an organization, let's explore a different case study that showcases a comprehensive approach to aligning internal culture with customer expectations.

Case Study: LEGO's Innovation Through Customer Engagement

LEGO, the world-renowned Danish toy company, has long been celebrated for its commitment to innovation, quality, and customer satisfaction. However, it's their strategic focus on fostering a deeply embedded customer-centric culture within their organization that truly sets them apart. This case study examines how LEGO has integrated customer feedback into every level of its operation, thereby enhancing its brand reputation and customer loyalty.

Strategy Implementation:

- Employee Engagement in Customer Feedback: LEGO encourages all employees, from designers to sales staff, to engage directly with customer feedback. This direct engagement helps employees understand the impact of their work on customer experiences and fosters a sense of ownership and responsibility towards improving those experiences.
- LEGO Ideas Platform: One of LEGO's most innovative customer engagement strategies is the LEGO Ideas platform, where customers can submit their own designs for new LEGO sets. This platform not only generates a wealth of ideas for new products but also deepens the relationship between LEGO and its customer base by making customers feel directly involved in the creation process.
- Cross-Functional Customer-Centric Teams: LEGO has established cross-functional teams that bring together employees from various departments to address specific customer feedback or work on projects aimed at enhancing

the customer experience. These teams operate with a high degree of autonomy, enabling quick and effective action based on customer insights.

Results:

- Enhanced Product Innovation: The direct line of communication between customers and all levels of the LEGO organization has led to numerous successful product launches, many of which originated from customer suggestions on the LEGO Ideas platform.
- Increased Customer Loyalty: LEGO's transparent and responsive approach to customer feedback has fostered a strong sense of community and loyalty among its customer base. This loyalty is reflected in the company's sustained growth and the strong performance of its new product lines.
- Employee Satisfaction and Brand Advocacy: Employees at LEGO report high levels of job satisfaction, stemming from their clear understanding of the impact of their work on customer happiness and the company's success. This satisfaction translates into strong internal brand advocacy, further enhancing LEGO's reputation.

LEGO's approach to building a customer-centric culture demonstrates the power of integrating customer feedback into every aspect of an organization's operations. By prioritizing the alignment of internal culture with external customer engagement strategies, LEGO has not only solidified its position as a leader in the toy industry but also set a benchmark for customer satisfaction and loyalty. This case study serves as a compelling example for other organizations striving to enhance their customer-centricity through active engagement and innovation.

Steps to Ensure Transformation

For the transformation into a customer-centric organization to be successful, creating the right internal culture is paramount. This process requires more than just superficial changes; it necessitates a deep, organization-wide commitment to understanding and acting on customer needs. Here are some considerations and conditions for success in this endeavor:

'**You have to genuinely believe in the value of putting the customer first.**' Implementing a customer-centric culture cannot be a mere checkbox exercise. It requires a fundamental belief in the value of customer satisfaction across all levels of the organization, from top leadership to frontline employees. Without this genuine belief, efforts to create a customer-centric culture may come across as inauthentic to both employees and customers, ultimately failing to achieve the desired impact.

'**If you do not integrate customer-centric values into every aspect of your operations, your efforts will fall short.**' Customer-centricity needs to be more than just a mission statement; it must be embedded into every process, policy, and decision made within the organization. This includes product development, marketing strategies, customer service protocols, and even the way internal meetings are conducted. Neglecting to fully integrate these values can lead to inconsistencies that customers will quickly notice, undermining trust and loyalty.

'This will not work, because assuming customer-centricity is only the responsibility of customer-facing roles is a mistake.' Every employee, regardless of their direct interaction with customers, impacts the customer experience. For example, a developer's approach to creating user-friendly software or an HR policy that supports employee wellbeing will indirectly affect customer satisfaction. Therefore, relegating customer-centricity to only those in direct contact with customers overlooks the broader impact of internal culture on the overall customer experience.

'If you do not measure and reward customer-centric behaviors, they will not become a part of your organization's DNA.' Recognizing and rewarding employees who demonstrate a commitment to customer satisfaction encourages those behaviors to proliferate throughout the organization. Without clear metrics for what constitutes customer-centric behavior, and without making those metrics a significant part of performance reviews and rewards systems, it's challenging to foster a culture that truly values and prioritizes the customer.

Creating the right internal culture for customer-centricity is an ongoing process that requires commitment, integration across all departments, accountability, and a system of reinforcement. By addressing these conditions, organizations can build a solid foundation for a culture that not only values customer satisfaction but also sees it as integral to the business's success.

TAKEAWAYS

So, what's your next step? Begin with an internal review. Engage with your teams, encourage open dialogues, and foster an environment where feedback is not only welcomed but valued. Then, take a proactive approach to customer feedback. Whether it's through surveys, direct communication channels, or social listening, ensure you have the means to listen and the agility to respond.

Make your organization an ecosystem that's a great place to work. Be that one employer that *everybody* wants to join. Don't build an environment that's toxic, or a culture where people are just there for the money and hate going to work every day. Instead, be the one place where people say, 'Oh, I'm not going to work. I'm actually going to a great place where I feel like this *isn't* work. This is my passion.'

We explored the concept that a customer-centric culture acts as the essential backbone of a humanized brand experience. By embedding customer-centric values deeply within the organization's DNA, companies can guarantee that their interactions with customers are consistently genuine, reflecting a true understanding and prioritization of customer needs and experiences. Such alignment enhances customer satisfaction, fostering a sense of loyalty and connection that transcends transactional relationships.

A great company has a supportive environment and a culture of happy people. We can add value to this by tapping into the emotional resonance of connections, which we'll explore in the next chapter.

CHAPTER 6

THE HEARTBEAT OF STORYTELLING

Emotionally Resonant Connections

Stories remain a timeless vessel for connecting in this day and age. When you share a story, anyone from any generation can relate to it—as long as it's authentic. In the earlier chapters, we talked about how authenticity is a key element when it comes to storytelling. When aiming to connect on an emotional level, be it in a seminar, a public speaking event, a panel, or a presentation, it's always advisable to share a *personal* story. Alternatively, offer a concrete example of anything you're trying to convince your audience of or convey to them.

This is what I mean when I say stories remain a timeless vessel for connecting. You connect immediately with someone who's telling you a story, because they're giving you something personal as a way of getting their message across. For example, start with: 'You know, the best color for laptops is usually black. Let me tell you a story ...'

Those six words—'Let me tell you a story'—are so powerful that you'll notice the audience actually sitting up and taking notice. As humans, we're wired for storytelling and geared to learn through stories. And that's how you link your message to a story. 'During the sudden Dubai floods that caused major chaos in early 2024, here's what happened ...'

STORYTELLING IS TIMELESS

Currently, everything you put on digital media stays there. If you look at any social media grid, personal or corporate brand, or even any product, it needs to have a story—because research showed that on digital media, people were looking at and relating to stories.

This is an important factor to look at in the branding space. Every brand needs a proper storyboard, a journey to showcase its values.

Let's say you tell a story about X, Y, or Z, with the objective of proving that black laptops are better than white ones. Each of these stories, whether they're delivered on a digital platform or a face-to-face platform at a public event, whether they're spoken one-on-one or in a meeting room with several people, will resonate with people. Stories always do.

You'll get your message heard loud and clear, but only if you use the power of storytelling.

Now, storytelling exists in many different shapes and forms, from an email to a presentation, from a proposal to an interview, from a massive public speaking event to a quiet one-to-one with your team or boss. Storytelling is extremely powerful because it resonates with the mind and the heart. (There's even neuroscientific evidence to back that up.)

Stories that resonate with your heart also activate your mind, and vice versa. Through telling a good story, you'll always be able to establish and build a strong connection between yourself and your target audience.

When we talk about the heartbeat of storytelling, we're referencing how to create a story, put a storyboard together, identify stories that align with your brand, and subtly integrate the message into your product or service.

Stories, in other words, enable selling without *really* selling. They do this by building a genuine connection with the human heart.

There's a structure to how you craft the perfect story. In the end, you want to hit two objectives. One is the connection you've established; the other is a call to action.

A story without a clear call to action is useless. On the other hand, if you tell a story with a definite call to action—whether it's to attract more followers, boost subscribers to your YouTube channel, entice people to buy your product, or remind them to sign that contract— that's what matters. Whether you're sending a simple reminder or a request to make a donation to charity, there *has* to be a call to action.

Successful stories conclude with a vivid call to action. When you're emotionally connected with that story, be it a 40-second video or a feature-length film, those emotions are urging you to *do* something. The best storytellers can guide you to exactly where that action is.

YOU CAN SPOT A FAKE

The raw and vulnerable connections that often come up in storytelling will resonate with your audience. So, it's not just about putting a promo together; it's about authentically connecting with your audience.

Customers nowadays have become very smart. Instead of believing anything they're told, they'll investigate. They're very skeptical towards entities, organizations, brands, and people in general. In today's world, everybody's trying to be an influencer and make money off you by streaming their videos, encouraging you to click 'Like', and suggesting you follow their various platforms. People, or even brands, have started looking into recruiting people who seem more 'authentic', who contrast with the unreal ones who do it for the fame game.

Brands used to affiliate with influencers and social media content creators. Nowadays they're asking: 'What's in it for me?' So, how are you generating leads? For example, if I hire an agency to promote my brand on social media, how do I measure the ROI? Brands have now started to closely guard their brand affiliation, because becoming associated with certain personalities may backfire on them.

People that are too controversial, or too 'out there', can affect the brand perception. Brands no longer take risks. They want to affiliate themselves with authentic people, those who seem genuine and grounded. It's no longer about cultivating the perfect image of a person who's completely unlike you and me.

Instead, the brands want to get the masses to look at them, which becomes a feeling of affiliation: 'If I'm going to look at your brand, I want to see *myself* within that brand. And if you bring me someone who doesn't look like me, then I can't resonate with your brand.' But with someone who's raw, vulnerable, real, and pure, the brand will be able to develop a loyal fanbase of followers.

CORPORATE OR PERSONAL BRAND

Every single one of us is a personal brand. Every single one of us has a unique identity, from those aged ten all the way to 100. You stand for a personal brand, which includes your values, principles, vision, and mission, as well as your goals, identity, and persona. By contrast, a *corporate* brand is a brand for an organization, a company, or an entity.

Because of our online presence in this day and age, each one of us develops a personal brand. It's up to the individual whether he or she wants to nurture their brand. It's like a plant. While it has a seed, it's up to each person how they nurture this plant in order for it to blossom into a beautiful tree.

You're represented by a series of pillars, combining values and purpose. Because everybody's unique, what matters to me might not really matter to you, and vice versa. More and more often, smart people are realizing that having a personal brand is key to their success.

In terms of how to spread your message, it's all about the impact you want to create.

A Powerful Message that Creates Social Awareness

There are many ways to build your message that aligns with your brand. For example, Ariel washing powder's 'Share the Load' campaign spread their message about women's empowerment across India via public service announcements. Those PSAs resonated with every woman, not just within India but across the globe. In the Asian and Arab world, we usually don't have that same 'Share the Load' experience. We're raised to be caregivers, wives, mothers, sisters, and daughters instead, bearing multiple responsibilities on our shoulders alone. Women's place has always been the home, but now that status quo is being changed by women choosing to go to work and build their careers.

It was this changing situation that helped make this PSA resonate with so many people—not only women, but also fathers, husbands, and the other male figures in women's lives.

This is the power of storytelling. It stays with you. You keep the story in your head and your heart and it never goes away. I can even visualize the scene. There's a living room and a TV and the father is sitting down. The man's daughter appears in the scene. (At this stage, we don't know she's his daughter.) The daughter has come home from work. She looks frazzled because she has to feed the kids and dinner is not prepared. As she trips on toys, her kids hang on to her. She has countless things to do. She's literally running around like a headless chicken. Her husband is on the PlayStation while her dad is watching TV.

We see the dad suddenly looking at his daughter, realizing what she's going through. While he behaved the same way with his wife, he couldn't bear seeing that his daughter has to handle the burden alone. This hits home. The father instinctively gets up from his seat.

While his daughter is putting some laundry in the washing machine, he places his hand on her shoulder and says in their own language, 'I'll share the load.'

That's where the concept of sharing the load comes from. When the individual is loading the washing machine, it's all about doing a routine chore, but it has additional layers of meaning.

So the announcement is selling Ariel washing powder. But Ariel's wider message is: 'We stand by women and gender equality, and we're raising awareness of the importance of men's role in sharing the load of responsibility for the household.'

Although every husband's wife has dreams, aspirations, and ambitions for a job or a career, she shouldn't be penalized for that. Instead, she should have a supportive partner who can actually give her wings to fly.

That's the power of storytelling.

Many brands are starting to get that. They're coming up with these kinds of social messages. It has to be tasteful and relevant to the region, though.

One can't take a PSA or a story or a way of thinking or a methodology from the USA and apply it verbatim to Egypt. It needs to relate to that certain sector of society. If the brand is targeting a middle-income audience, they need to relate to their lifestyle. You can't hire someone who carries a Louis Vuitton handbag for a PR campaign targeted to those in the low-income bracket. These are the types of perceptions a brand needs to be sensitive about. Your brand campaign needs to be relevant and sensitive to the local community, traditions, culture, language, and so on.

Know Your Audience

Before starting any PR campaign, it's necessary to research the segment of society you want to target, taking into account the geographical location and culture. What works in Morocco might not work in the UAE, and vice versa. Again, we're going back to the same point that I have mentioned before: One size does *not* fit all.

We have to redefine personal branding. I can't create a personal branding plan for my client who's an entrepreneur, then take the same personal brand and apply it to an athlete in London. It won't be successful. We have to be agile enough to anticipate the needs of our clients. We have to be ever-receptive to the changing generations to be aware of what's happening in the world, especially in the Digital Age as well. Each generation is different, so you constantly need to lift your game.

And while one size doesn't fit all, there are certain values that no one will disagree on: motherhood, sisterhood, womanhood. These are universal. Equality is another. There are values that everyone stands for. Including them within your overarching message will have an effect on the audience.

If we break down the details, it has to be segmented according to the communities and your specific audience.

This exploration into storytelling is more than a guide to better marketing; it's an invitation to rekindle the age-old tradition of sharing stories, reminding us of the power of narratives to move, to connect, and to transform.

DEFINING CORE VALUES AND ADVOCACIES

For the Corporate Brand:

Identifying and clearly articulating the core values and mission of your organization is the starting point. These values act as the North Star, guiding every facet of your business operations—from product development to customer engagement and beyond. For example, a technology firm might champion innovation, user empowerment, and digital inclusivity. These core values should be palpable in every communication, product, and service, ensuring that they resonate authentically with your audience.

For the Personal Brand:

The journey here is inward, requiring introspection and honesty. What drives you? What are the causes close to your heart? This could range from advocating for gender equality, to championing environmental sustainability, to fostering educational accessibility. Your personal brand should be a mirror reflecting your deepest convictions and how you interact with the world around you. It's about marrying your passions with your actions in a way that is both genuine and impactful.

CRAFTING AN IMPACT THROUGH AUTHENTICITY

In the Corporate Realm:

Your corporate brand's impact is directly proportional to how authentically you can manifest your stated values in your business practices. If sustainability is a cornerstone value, then your operational footprint should reflect this commitment. It's about walking the talk—implementing eco-friendly practices, for example, and then sharing these stories of commitment and impact with your audience through various channels like social media, sustainability reports, and community engagement.

On a Personal Level:

Here, the impact is more intimate, more direct. It's about how you, as an individual, embody and advocate for your beliefs. Whether it's through volunteering, content creation, or public speaking, your actions and stories should serve as beacons that not only illuminate the causes you care about but also mobilize and inspire others. It's your authenticity that will resonate, drawing people to your cause and amplifying your impact.

SPREADING YOUR MESSAGE

Through the Corporate Lens:

Utilize your corporate platform to champion the messages that align with your brand's ethos. Launch initiatives, campaigns, or public service announcements that tackle the issues you stand for. The 'Share the Load' campaign is a prime example, challenging entrenched gender stereotypes by encouraging shared household responsibilities. These campaigns not only spotlight the issue but also position your brand as a catalyst for change.

From a Personal Perspective:

Your personal channels are your pulpit. Use them to advocate, educate, and inspire. Share content that not only highlights the issues you are passionate about but also engages and provokes thought. Your personal experiences and journeys, shared authentically, can be powerful catalysts for conversation and change.

THE ART OF PERSONAL STORYTELLING

For Corporates:

While a corporation may not share personal stories in the traditional sense, it can and should share narratives of its stakeholders— employees, customers, and community members—who embody the brand's values. These stories serve to humanize the brand, making its values tangible and relatable to the audience.

For Individuals:

This is where the power of personal storytelling truly shines. Share your journey, the challenges you've faced, the battles you've fought, and the lessons you've learned. Authenticity is key. Your vulnerability, when shared judiciously, can forge connections that transcend the superficial, creating deep and meaningful engagement with your audience.

BALANCING REVELATION WITH PROFESSIONALISM

In a Corporate Context:

Transparency breeds trust. Let your audience see behind the curtain—show them the work you're doing, the challenges you're facing, and the strides you're making towards your goals. This not only builds credibility but also engenders loyalty by making your audience feel like they're part of your journey.

On a Personal Note:

Navigating the delicate equilibrium between personal revelation and professionalism in branding is akin to walking a tightrope. It's about knowing how much to share, when to share it, and the context in which your stories are unfolded. This balance is pivotal, especially in the realm of personal branding, where the lines between the personal and professional selves often blur.

The goal is to be open and authentic, sharing your failures and successes, doubts and certainties, in a manner that not only humanizes you but also elevates your brand. But how does one achieve this delicate balance? Let's delve deeper.

Authenticity with Purpose

Being authentic means sharing your true self with your audience, but not all aspects of one's personal life serve a purpose in building a professional brand. Select stories and experiences that have shaped your professional outlook, underscored your resilience, or highlighted a learning curve. These narratives should serve a dual purpose: showcasing your human side and reinforcing the values or skills that define your professional brand.

Professional Vulnerability

The concept of vulnerability in professional settings is often seen as a risk, yet when executed with thoughtfulness, it can be a powerful tool for connection. Sharing challenges you've faced or mistakes you've made can be incredibly relatable, fostering a sense of trust and authenticity. However, it's crucial to frame these stories in a way that focuses on growth and learning rather than dwelling on the negatives. Your aim should be to demonstrate how these experiences have contributed to your professional development and how they inform your approach to challenges today.

Curate Your Narrative

In the Digital Age, where personal information can easily become public, curating the narrative you share is more important than ever. This doesn't mean fabricating a persona but rather carefully selecting the aspects of your personal journey that contribute positively to your professional image. Consider what your stories convey about your character, work ethic, and values. Each piece of your narrative should add depth to your brand, showing your audience not just who you are but who you aspire to be as a professional.

Engage with Intent

Engagement is a two-way street. As you share your stories, also take the time to listen and interact with your audience. This interaction can provide valuable insights into what resonates with them, allowing you to tailor your content accordingly. However, maintain a level of professionalism in these engagements. The way you respond to comments, handle criticism, and participate in discussions should consistently reflect the professionalism and respect that are core to your brand.

Set Boundaries

Finally, setting boundaries is essential for maintaining the balance between personal revelation and professionalism. Decide early on what aspects of your personal life are off-limits and stick to these boundaries. It's okay to keep certain parts of your life private, as this not only protects your personal space but also ensures that your professional brand remains focused and relevant to your audience.

In essence, the balance between personal revelation and professionalism in branding is not about limiting what you share but about sharing with intention and purpose. It's about constructing a narrative that is authentic, engaging, and reflective of your professional journey and aspirations. By doing so, you not only enrich your personal brand but also build deeper, more meaningful connections with your audience, laying the foundation for a brand that is both relatable and respected.

Nike's Storytelling Mastery

Nike exemplifies how to weave storytelling into the fabric of branding. Their campaigns often feature stories of determination, such as the journey of a novice runner or the relentless pursuit of excellence by a world-renowned athlete. These narratives are carefully crafted to align with Nike's 'Just Do It' ethos, encouraging consumers to overcome their own obstacles. By focusing on the emotional journey rather than the product, Nike builds a powerful emotional connection with its audience.

Richard Branson's Personal Branding

Richard Branson's personal brand is a testament to the power of blending professional achievements with personal experiences. His stories of adventure, risk-taking, and overcoming adversity not only humanize him but also reinforce the adventurous spirit of the Virgin brand. Branson's approachable and relatable manner, combined with his business acumen, creates a compelling narrative that attracts followers and customers alike.

Procter & Gamble's Emotional Storytelling

P&G's ability to touch on universal human experiences makes its storytelling exceptionally effective. Their 'Thank You, Mom' campaign, for instance, celebrated the unsung heroes behind Olympic athletes—their mothers—thereby evoking deep emotional responses from the audience. By tapping into fundamental emotions such as love, gratitude, and perseverance, P&G fosters a powerful emotional bond with consumers, transcending the traditional advertiser–consumer relationship.

In weaving these narratives, these brands and individuals demonstrate the profound impact of storytelling in building brand equity and fostering loyalty. Through a blend of personal revelation and professionalism, they engage audiences on a deeper level, turning consumers into brand advocates and followers into a community. This strategic approach to storytelling not only enriches the brand's narrative but also solidifies its place in the competitive market landscape, proving that the stories we tell are as crucial as the products we sell.

Effectiveness Tips

To ensure the effectiveness of storytelling and personal branding strategies, it's paramount that these approaches are meticulously planned and strategically executed. The success of these initiatives hinges on several critical factors and conditions, each tailored to address potential challenges and objections. Here's an expanded perspective, incorporating additional tools and considerations for a comprehensive strategy.

1. 'Engage in active audience research and segmentation.'

Understanding your audience goes beyond surface-level demographics. It involves deep research into their behaviors, preferences, cultural nuances, and challenges. Tools like surveys, social media analytics, and focus groups can provide invaluable insights into what resonates with your audience. This research should inform every aspect of your storytelling, ensuring that your narratives are not just heard but felt on a personal level.

2. 'If you do not tailor your messaging to be relevant to your region and local community, your strategy may fail to engage your intended audience.'

Localization of content is crucial for connecting with your audience on a meaningful level. Utilize tools like geo-targeting in digital campaigns and local insights to customize your messaging. Stories that reflect local realities, challenges, and triumphs can significantly increase your brand's relevance and resonance within a community.

3. 'This strategy will not work because a one-size-fits-all approach to storytelling can dilute your brand's impact.'

To avoid the pitfalls of a generic approach, employ content customization and personalization tools. CRM (Customer

Relationship Management) systems and AI-driven content platforms can help you deliver tailored stories to different segments of your audience, based on their interactions and preferences. Being strategic and aligned with your brand values in every story you tell ensures that your narrative strengthens your brand identity rather than watering it down.

4. 'For this to work, you have to effectively communicate your brand values in every story you share.'

Your brand values are the compass that guides your storytelling. Every narrative should be a reflection of these values, communicated in a way that is both authentic and engaging. Tools like storytelling workshops for your team and brand storytelling templates can ensure consistency and authenticity across all communications. This alignment reinforces your brand's identity and fosters trust with your audience.

5. 'If you do not leverage the right platforms to share your stories, you risk missing your target audience.'

The choice of platform is as critical as the story itself. Whether it's social media, blogs, podcasts, or traditional media, selecting the right channels depends on where your audience spends their time. Analytics tools can provide insights into audience preferences and behaviors, helping you make informed decisions about where to invest your storytelling efforts.

6. 'Neglecting feedback loops can lead to missed opportunities for connection and improvement.'

Active listening and engagement with your audience are crucial. Tools like social listening platforms and feedback mechanisms allow you to gauge reactions to your stories, providing opportunities for real-time engagement and adaptation. This feedback loop is essential for refining your approach and ensuring your storytelling remains relevant and resonant.

7. 'Be prepared to iterate and evolve your storytelling strategy based on changing audience needs and market dynamics.'

The landscape in which your brand operates will change—and with it, so must your storytelling. Tools for market analysis and trend forecasting can help you anticipate shifts in consumer behavior and preferences, allowing your brand to remain relevant and engaged with its audience. Embracing flexibility and adaptability in your storytelling strategy ensures that your brand can navigate changes without losing its core identity.

TAKEAWAYS

The impact of your brand—how it influences individuals, communities, and even broader societal issues—further solidifies your brand equity. For corporate brands, this might mean initiating sustainability programs, supporting social causes, or fostering innovation that benefits society. For personal brands, it could involve advocating for issues you are passionate about, sharing knowledge, or contributing to community projects. These actions demonstrate a commitment to making a positive difference, elevating your brand in the eyes of your audience.

Moreover, spreading your message in a way that resonates with your audience requires a deep understanding of their needs, aspirations, and challenges. Crafting stories that reflect these aspects, sharing testimonials that highlight the impact of your brand, and demonstrating a genuine commitment to your values can create emotional connections that are much more robust and enduring than any transactional relationship.

In every communication and every story, embed a call to action: visit our website, join a movement, change your mindset, donate, buy our product, follow our account ... whatever it is, make sure it's clear.

To emotionally connect with the audience, this process requires a strategy that involves extensive research and creative storytelling. This leads us to the next chapter about the importance of authentic storytelling.

CHAPTER 7

AUTHENTIC ENGAGEMENT

Crafting Powerful Narratives

Brands that simply explain what their product is, but have no story behind it, don't stand apart from their competition. A powerful story adds value to any brand, which also means authenticity comes from a place of uniqueness.

So, how can one make a brand or a person stand out by being authentic?

It all starts with a story.

The story can be about the struggles endured by a brand's founder, which explains the 'why' behind the brand and what the brand stands for. This encompasses their values, the objective that the brand is trying to achieve for the community, the customer, and the world at large. One example is Nike. For the longest time, Nike has stood out for athletes with dreams and aspirations. The 'Just Do It' slogan stems from that idea, which contains three layers.

The slogan's first layer revolves around the company's sponsorship of brand ambassadors from less privileged communities and humble backgrounds, who've made it big as athletes—in other words, underdog stories.

The second layer is about promoting wellness and fitness, with the tagline conveying 'Just Get Up and Do It.' This means just run, get fit, play basketball. Just be active. Don't wait.

A brand like Nike has a vivid third layer that's easy to associate yourself with, containing a clear message that makes the brand memorable.

STANDING OUT IN A CROWDED MARKETPLACE

The message behind the brand needs to be powerful. Otherwise, the story won't achieve what it needs to achieve. For Nike, the messaging encourages people to just get up and get active. Whether you're an entrepreneur, an athlete, a mother, an executive, or a child, just do it and dream big. Make it happen.

Nike ads show a child running in the rain or pushing herself as a gymnast, then showing her mother waking her up at 4:00 a.m. to practice. The message is all about fulfilling your dreams, working hard, and pushing your boundaries.

The messaging here is very authentic and relatable to everyone's life.

Why are the message and story important? They help you resonate with the message emotionally and mentally. For example, a Nike ad talks about a little girl whose dream since age five was to become an Olympic gymnast. Watching it, you go through the stages and milestones of what *she* had to go through to reach that far, triggering emotions and ensuring the story resonates with the audience. This inspires you to buy Nike products, because it makes you feel as if wearing them will help you achieve anything in the world. This forms a connection with hearts and minds, influencing your mood beyond the 90-second ad or even the 40-second social media reel.

It's all about how it makes you feel, because heartfelt connections are powerful.

This emotional connection comes from the message that inspires. Stories like these ones tap into emotions, making it easier for the customer to make an emotional connection with the brand. This emotional bond can be a very strong driver of brand loyalty. And as marketers always say, it can definitely influence the purchasing decision.

For the longest time, Nike resonated with my son (who's a football player), because the football player Ronaldo featured in their ads and promos. Recently, he switched to Puma for his football sneakers, because Puma is more comfortable for his type of feet. Yet his other sneakers have all been Nike, because the brand resonates with him.

These authentic stories build brand trust and create differentiation. Why is Nike different from Adidas or Puma or Skechers? It's the story told by the messaging that creates brand differentiation in a very crowded market. Brands need to be unique, telling authentic stories that can really stand out from competitors.

This clever messaging allows the brand to highlight their unique values and characteristics. The key characteristic of Nike is articulating that 'Just Do It' attitude, then making it stand out to consumers. What are you waiting for? You know what I mean?

It's a similar story with Procter & Gamble versus Unilever, or Pampers versus Huggies. One brand of diapers resonated with me, because purchasing one pack equaled one vaccine delivered to a child in need. This connected with me on a personal level. And why did Pampers do this? It was a strategic decision, because

Pampers knew their target audience: parents. Giving a child a chance to live connects with a parent. The brand clearly knew their audience, developing a narrative with a very powerful emotional connection.

Essential Ingredients for Authentic Storytelling

This recipe encompasses:

sincerity, where honesty in sharing triumphs and tribulations fosters trust

vulnerability, which allows audiences to see their reflections in your story

passion, the driving force that infuses your narrative with energy

personal truth, anchoring your story in genuine experiences

and **engagement**, the art of speaking directly to the heart of your audience.

Now, imagine two brands launching their campaigns simultaneously. One opts for a glossy high-octane advertisement devoid of any genuine narrative or connection to its ethos. Despite its visual appeal, it barely scratches the surface of the audience's consciousness. The other brand chooses a different path, sharing a raw, unvarnished story of its origins, the hurdles it faced, and how it triumphed over adversity. This narrative, though less polished, strikes a chord, resonating deeply with the audience. The stark difference in the impact of these approaches underscores a fundamental truth: Authenticity is essential to forming connections and attaining credibility in today's digital world.

Authentic storytelling becomes not just a strategy but a necessity for building trust and establishing a genuine connection with our audience. It is through these truthful narratives that brands can forge a credible identity, one that is embraced and championed by their audience.

To navigate this shift effectively, it is imperative to embrace authenticity in every facet of our storytelling.

BUILDING TRUST

Creating an emotional connection creates differentiation in the consumer's mind, which then enhances the brand identity. This identity will always be associated with certain drives, values, and emotions, encouraging engagement. Through highlighting certain posts and comments on social media, the brand starts fostering a community of followers.

For example, a Nike person will never buy a brand other than Nike. Recently, the author started wearing New Balance, but Nike is still a favorite brand. By making an emotional connection on social media, the company can make it a comfort for people to buy the product.

Creating long-term value is another benefit of authentic storytelling, which involves building a sustainable brand with a message that endures through generations. From the moment Michael Jordan was made Nike's brand ambassador, their powerful association echoed all the way to the next generation. Brands develop a loyal customer base by genuinely connecting with a famous face who has a compelling story. A single association can continue through different generations and phases of growth.

So, being a teenaged Michael Jordan fan who played basketball automatically turned me into a Nike fan. When I'm buying shoes for my kids, where am I going to go? I'm going to go to Nike. And eventually, either they'll grow up to love Nike or switch brands, depending on those other brands' authentic storytelling.

It's all about what you stand for, including your values and principles. *What's your message? What's your message?* Keep drilling this into people's heads. Every brand has to have a message. Because the Nike logo is so familiar, it causes the brand to automatically resonate with people.

The Name Became the Noun

In Egypt, we grew up saying, 'I'm going to go and make myself a Nescafé.' Coffee is synonymous with Nescafé. It's the same thing with tea, where many say, 'I'm going to make a Lipton.' This kind of brand association becomes generational.

And when you say, 'I don't have detergent,' we in India say, 'I don't have Ariel.' It just comes up, enduring from generation to generation. And if the brand is clever, with great marketers who understand the market well, they can build that brand loyalty for life. (That is, unless something drastic happens and the brand is criticized for their sustainability or environmental policies.)

Crafting Impactful Stories

1. Define the Core Message

In-Depth Analysis:

The core message serves as the foundation of your storytelling efforts. It encapsulates what you want your audience to understand, feel, and remember about your brand. This message should be a reflection of your brand's values and mission, distilled into a simple yet powerful statement. For example, if your brand values sustainability, your core message could focus on the importance of preserving natural resources for future generations.

Strategies for Development:

Value Alignment: Conduct workshops or brainstorming sessions with key stakeholders to ensure the core message aligns with your brand's values and mission.

Simplicity and Clarity: Refine your message to ensure it's simple, clear, and easily understandable. Avoid jargon and complex language.

Emotional Connection: Infuse your core message with emotional elements that resonate with your target audience, making it not just a statement but a call to action that evokes a strong response.

2. Identify the Story

In-Depth Analysis:

Selecting the right story is crucial. It must be a genuine reflection of your core message, demonstrating your brand's values in action. Real-life examples, such as community projects, customer success stories, or behind-the-scenes looks at your company's processes, provide tangible evidence of your brand's commitment to its values.

Strategies for Selection:

Authenticity Check: Ensure the story is true and accurately represents real events or initiatives. Authenticity cannot be fabricated.

Impact Highlighting: Choose stories that have a clear impact, whether it's on individuals, communities, or the environment. This impact should directly relate to your core message.

Diversity and Inclusion: Consider stories that showcase diversity and inclusion, reflecting the broad spectrum of your audience and community.

3. Storyboard Development

In-Depth Analysis:

A storyboard is a visual and textual representation of your story, laying out each key moment. It's a planning tool that helps visualize the narrative flow and identify the essential elements of your story. This includes the setting, characters, conflict, action, and resolution.

Strategies for Creation:

Visual Mapping: Use a mix of sketches, text, and notes to map out the narrative, ensuring a logical flow that builds towards a compelling resolution.

Feedback Loops: Involve different team members in the storyboard review process to gather diverse perspectives and insights, which can enhance the story's depth and appeal.

Emotional Journey: Pay special attention to the emotional journey you want your audience to experience, mapping out how each segment of the story contributes to this journey.

4. Content Creation

In-Depth Analysis:

Creating content from your storyboard involves translating your visual and textual outline into a fully realized narrative. This can take various forms, including written stories, videos, podcasts, or social media posts. The content should be engaging, visually appealing, and reflective of the story's authenticity.

Strategies for Development:

Multimedia Integration: Use a combination of text, images, videos, and audio to tell your story, catering to different preferences and enhancing engagement.

Narrative Voice: Ensure the narrative voice and tone are consistent with your brand's identity and resonate with your target audience.

Accuracy and Detail: Include specific details and accurate descriptions to enhance the story's authenticity and immersion.

5. Distribution and Engagement

In-Depth Analysis:

Effective Distributions: Ensures that your story reaches your intended audience through the right channels. Engagement is about fostering interaction with your story, encouraging comments, shares, and discussions that amplify its reach and impact.

Strategies for Execution:

Channel Selection: Identify the most appropriate platforms for your story based on where your target audience is most active and engaged.

Cross-Promotion: Utilize multiple channels for promotion to ensure broad exposure, including social media, email newsletters, your website, and even offline methods.

Interactive Elements: Incorporate questions, calls to action, or interactive elements within your story to encourage audience participation and feedback.

By following these detailed steps and employing strategic planning at each stage, you can craft authentic stories that not only showcase your brand's values and achievements but also deeply resonate with your audience, fostering a sense of community and shared purpose.

VALUES THAT MATTER

As each consumer's life progresses, social and environmental governance often become key elements of a brand. To progress with generations to come, each brand has to learn to 'ride the wave', adjusting their message to suit current trends. The new generations won't come on board if the company's values don't gel with their own—but as long as the brand is reinventing itself, it will be recognized and valued.

To succeed, brands need to be able to approach each younger generation with relevant, relatable, and authentic stories aligned with their core values. This creates an unbreakable bond between the brand and the audience.

So, when aiming to create something similar, recognize the value of storytelling and learn to apply it in the digital world.

Creating engaging digital experiences is a complex approach, especially when you want to form lasting human connections in the digital realm. To find out more, let's get deeper into a world that's rapidly heading online.

Prerequisites to Creating an Authentic Story

For authentic storytelling to effectively elevate your brand and foster deep connections with your audience, several critical conditions must be met, and potential pitfalls must be carefully navigated. Here's an expanded exploration of the prerequisites for success and responses to common objections in the realm of authentic storytelling:

1. Ensure Actions Align with Stories

The integrity of your storytelling initiative hinges on the alignment between your narratives and your brand's actions. Authentic storytelling transcends mere narrative craftsmanship; it requires a lived experience of the values and missions your stories seek to convey. Discrepancies between what you profess in your stories and what your brand practices in reality can lead to a credibility crisis.

2. Avoid Riding the Wave of Someone Else's Story

In an era where trends and viral stories dominate the digital landscape, it's tempting to hitch your brand's narrative wagon to these fleeting stars. However, unless there's a genuine connection to your brand's core identity and values, such attempts can backfire, painting your brand as opportunistic or inauthentic.

3. Navigating Copyright Considerations

The authenticity of your storytelling can be undermined by legal and ethical challenges if copyright considerations are not meticulously observed. Utilizing copyrighted material without permission or proper attribution can lead to legal repercussions and damage your brand's reputation for integrity.

4. Avoid Perceptions of Inauthenticity

Striving for authenticity can sometimes lead brands to overcompensate, resulting in narratives that feel forced or insincere. The audience today is highly discerning and can easily detect when a brand is 'trying too hard' to appear authentic, which can erode trust and engagement.

5. Selecting the Right Messaging

The cornerstone of effective storytelling is the selection of messages that resonate deeply with both your brand identity and your audience's values. Misalignment or mixed messages can confuse your audience and dilute your brand's impact.

Successfully navigating the complex landscape of authentic storytelling demands a strategic approach that prioritizes genuine alignment between actions and narratives, respects copyright laws, and engages audiences with sincerity.

TAKEAWAYS

1. Be Real: Embrace the authenticity at the core of your brand. Reflect on the stories that truly represent who you are and what you stand for. Moving forward, commit to sharing these stories with honesty and vulnerability. Let your audience see the real faces behind your brand, the challenges you've overcome, and the victories you've celebrated. This authenticity is what will resonate most deeply with your audience, turning casual observers into loyal advocates.

2. Recognize Your Values: Take a moment to clearly articulate and reaffirm your brand's core values. These values should be the guiding star for every piece of content you create, every story you tell, and every interaction you have with your audience. Consider how these values are reflected in your current storytelling efforts and identify any gaps or misalignments.

The journey from traditional to digital storytelling is not just about changing platforms but about embracing the possibilities of new narratives, new engagements, and new connections. It's about leveraging the digital world to further cement the unbreakable bond between your brand and your audience, ensuring that every click, every view, and every share is a step deeper into the shared story that binds you together.

CHAPTER 8

CREATING ENGAGING DIGITAL EXPERIENCES

Human Connection in the Digital Realm

We're living in a new world where almost everyone is aware of or using AI. We can't ignore this technology, including how it could help us evolve.

How does one humanize AI for a brand while aligning it with a message?

AI is a tool. Therefore, the optimal way to use it is just as everyone uses social media. AI can be applied in an intelligent way, so it works for us instead of us working for *it*. There are definitely significant advantages in why companies or brands would adopt and integrate AI to enhance their customer experience.

For example, AI could be useful in researching and analyzing data, crucial in understanding individual customer preferences and behaviors. Instead of hiring a research team, AI helps brands tailor their marketing messages, product recommendations, and services to meet the specific needs of each customer.

The chapter will guide you through innovative strategies and practical examples of how brands can harness the power of digital tools—from artificial intelligence to social media platforms—to create experiences that feel personal, engaging, and deeply human. We will explore how storytelling, user experience design, and interactive technologies can be synergistically employed to create digital spaces where genuine connections flourish.

AI SUPPORTS BRANDING

Used correctly, AI tools would enhance customer experiences and increase engagement. With AI, we can gather data faster than humans alone, improving the brand's ability to develop their messages. In this sense, human resources can be applied in the most creative way. Instead of a team being tasked with understanding and collecting data, they'll now build strategies in accordance with the data that the AI has analyzed and personalized for the brand.

Besides phase one of personalization, customer service is another key benefit. The second phase of customer service involves AI-powered chatbots and virtual assistants to guide you through complex processes around the clock—24/7 customer service. These bots answer questions, solve problems, offer assistance, and so on, with endurance that's not humanly possible.

The third phase of customer service actually involves having a face-to-face or a human-to-human connection. For example, when you make a call to the bank, the first or second phase involves AI or virtual assistance. You then ask for a customer representative to address your specific need.

Any kind of service starts with the AI tool. After the company has understood the customer's complaints or needs, AI analyzes the situation and offers workable solutions where possible. If the issue is resolved, there's no need to speak to a human.

This saves time and energy, lifting the financial burden of hiring extra staff while saving time.

As a result, your employees can be involved in more creative projects. (AI works best in predictable analytical tasks.)

Awareness of the Digital World

In today's Digital Age, where the sheer volume of content can seem overwhelming, the critical question that stands between a piece of content being scrolled past or making a meaningful impact is, 'What's In It For Me?' (WIIFM). We will explore the profound significance of this question, illustrating why a deep understanding and application of this principle is necessary for anyone engaged in the creation of digital content, be it for personal enhancement or corporate branding. The essence of this inquiry lies in forging genuine connections that resonate with the audience's core desires and needs.

Reflect for a moment on the content that has truly captured your attention in the past. It's likely that such content went beyond mere information dissemination; it spoke to you on a personal level, offering insights, inspiration, or solutions that were directly relevant to your life or work. This chapter is dedicated to dissecting the elements that contribute to creating such impactful content. By focusing on the WIIFM factor from the perspective of your audience, you will learn how to craft content that not only stands out in a crowded digital landscape but also creates lasting engagement, transforming passive consumers into active participants in your brand's narrative.

MBC Academy: Fostering Talents in Film and Media

With MBC Academy, we aimed to harness and develop talents in Saudi Arabia's film and media industries, along with empowering youth across various fields. We launched the 'Talent Nurture' campaign, which focused on practical and theatrical techniques to effectively develop skills and talents. By offering hands-on workshops, mentorship programs, and real-world project opportunities, we equipped young individuals with the tools they needed to succeed. This approach not only amplified our reach but also strengthened our relationship with our audience, both on screen and on digital platforms.

Get Started

1. Evaluate Your Digital Platforms: Begin by conducting a thorough review of your website, social media profiles, and any other digital touchpoints your brand has. Assess them for user-friendliness and accessibility. Ensure that navigation is intuitive, content is easily discoverable, and your platforms are inclusive, catering to users with diverse needs. Make necessary optimizations to offer a seamless experience that encourages longer engagement times and fosters a positive brand perception.

2. Devise Strategies for Authentic Engagement: Shift your focus to social media, where the heart of digital engagement lies. Craft a strategy that prioritizes authentic interaction with your audience. This involves going beyond scheduled posts and advertisements to include real-time conversations, responses to comments, and participation in relevant trends and discussions. Showcase the human side of your brand by sharing behind-the-scenes content,

employee stories, customer testimonials, and other relatable content that resonates with your audience on a personal level.

3. Explore AI Integration: Consider the strategic integration of chatbots and virtual assistants on your digital platforms. These AI-driven tools can significantly enhance the efficiency and responsiveness of your customer support. Start by identifying the most common inquiries or support requests your brand receives and program your AI tools to provide accurate, helpful responses. However, ensure there's a balance—while AI can handle routine queries, complex or sensitive issues should be escalated to human customer service representatives to maintain that crucial element of human touch.

4. Distinguish Authentic from Fake Engagement: In your efforts to engage with your audience, remain vigilant against the pitfalls of fake engagement. Authentic engagement is characterized by meaningful interactions that add value to your audience's experience with your brand. In contrast, fake engagement, often manifested through purchased likes, comments, or followers, offers no real value and can damage your brand's credibility. Focus on building genuine relationships with your audience through quality content and sincere interaction.

By taking these steps, you will enhance your brand's digital presence and deepen the connection with your audience, paving the way for a more engaged, loyal community. Remember, the goal is to create digital experiences that are not just seen but felt, making every interaction with your brand memorable and meaningful.

The Successful Brand Stories

Let's look at the journeys of Apple and Wendy's, brands which provide clear insights into creating engaging digital experiences that resonate with audiences on a deeply personal level. These brands have navigated the digital realm with distinct strategies, showcasing the versatility and impact of well-executed content and engagement approaches.

Apple: The Epitome of Emotional Storytelling and Innovation

Apple stands apart in demonstrating how a brand can weave technology with storytelling to capture hearts and minds worldwide. Its success in the digital space is a product of innovative technology and an ability to connect with users on an emotional level, demonstrating the transformative power of its products in everyday life.

- Narrative-Driven Product Launches: Apple's product launches are examples of narrative-driven marketing. Each event is crafted like a story, with a buildup, climax, and resolution, showcasing the product not merely as a gadget but as a catalyst for change, creativity, and connection. The digital broadcast of these events allows Apple to reach a global audience, making each launch a momentous occasion that people look forward to.
- Emotional Resonance Through Advertising: Apple's advertisements are meticulously designed to evoke emotions, whether joy, nostalgia, or hope. By highlighting real-life uses of its products—from capturing precious moments with an iPhone camera to creating music on a MacBook—Apple's content

has evolved from traditional advertising to embody relatable narratives that reflect the experiences and aspirations of its users.

- Community Engagement via User-Generated Content: Apple leverages social media to encourage users to share their own stories and creations made with Apple products. Campaigns like 'Shot on iPhone' showcase the capabilities of the iPhone camera and celebrates the creativity of the Apple community, creating a shared space for users to inspire and be inspired.

Wendy's: Mastering Engagement with Boldness and Humor

Wendy's has redefined the playbook for brand engagement on social media with its audacious and humorous tone. Wendy's embraced a bold strategy that emphasizes personality, making it one of the most talked-about brands online.

- Wit and Banter on X (Twitter): Wendy's Twitter account is renowned for its sharp wit and readiness to engage in playful banter, not just with customers but also with competitors. This approach has transformed its digital presence into a source of entertainment, drawing in followers who look forward to the brand's next tweet.
- Active and Relatable Engagement: Beyond witty replies, Wendy's maintains a high level of engagement by participating in current trends, memes, and social conversations. This active presence keeps the brand relevant and relatable, fostering a sense of camaraderie with its audience.

- Creative Campaigns that Spark Conversations: From roasting competitors in a mixtape to challenging followers to win a year's supply of chicken nuggets, Wendy's creates campaigns that spark conversations and encourage widespread engagement. These initiatives increase brand visibility and strengthens its image as a brand that's dynamic and fun.

The digital success stories of Apple and Wendy's highlight several key lessons for brands aiming to make a mark in the Digital Age. Apple demonstrates the unparalleled power of emotional storytelling and the importance of showcasing product impact on human experiences. Wendy's, on the other hand, illustrates the effectiveness of engaging with audiences through a distinctive brand voice that's bold and humorous.

Both strategies, while different in their execution, highlight the importance of authenticity, creativity, and audience understanding in crafting digital content that stands out. For brands looking to enhance their digital presence, the journeys of Apple and Wendy's offer valuable blueprints for creating content that not only reaches but also deeply engages and delights the audience, paving the way for lasting connections and brand loyalty in the digital marketplace.

CONDITIONS FOR SUCCESS

For the strategies outlined to truly work and for a brand to stand out in the digital realm, several conditions must be met, and potential objections should be carefully considered. Here's a deeper look into what it takes to ensure the effectiveness of your digital content strategy:

1. 'Prioritize the user experience.'

A stellar digital presence hinges on how well a brand can engage its audience. This means creating a user experience (UX) that is not only intuitive and easy to navigate but also enjoyable. Every touchpoint, from your website to your social media platforms, should be designed with the user in mind, making information accessible, interactions smooth, and content engaging. Failure to prioritize UX can lead to a disconnect with your audience, reducing the impact of even the most well-crafted content.

2. 'If you do not blend seamlessly, your efforts might not yield the desired impact.'

In the context of digital marketing, blending seamlessly refers to the integration of various content forms across multiple platforms while maintaining a consistent brand voice and identity. If your content strategy lacks this seamless integration, there's a risk of fragmenting your brand message, leading to confusion among your audience. A disjointed brand experience can dilute your marketing efforts, making it difficult to build a strong, recognizable brand presence online.

3. 'Create a fine balance to ensure that the genuine human connection is maintained.'

In the rush to digitize and automate, brands may lose sight of the essence of why people connect with content in the first place— the human element. Without a fine balance between leveraging technology and maintaining genuine human interaction, digital content strategies risk becoming impersonal and ineffective. Engagement is not just about clicks and views; it's about creating a sense of community and belonging among your audience. If your digital strategy overlooks the importance of human connection, it may fail to resonate deeply with your audience, limiting its ability to build lasting relationships and loyalty.

Successfully implementing a digital content strategy that captivates and retains your audience requires more than just following trends and using the right keywords. It demands a commitment to creating a superior user experience, ensuring seamless integration across all digital platforms, and, most importantly, fostering genuine human connections. By addressing these conditions and preemptively tackling potential objections, brands can create digital experiences that not only engage but also endure, turning viewers into advocates and customers into community.

This involves a sophisticated dance of leveraging cutting-edge technology to enhance, rather than erode, the human element of brand interactions.

Technology, when thoughtfully applied, has the potential to amplify human connections rather than diminish them. The digital realm offers unparalleled opportunities to engage with audiences across the globe, transcending physical limitations to foster a sense of closeness and community. Yet, the challenge lies in ensuring that these digital experiences do not become cold and impersonal but instead resonate with the warmth, empathy, and authenticity that define meaningful human interactions. Using AI technology minimizes the energy and time required to complete the grunt work of research and studies, along with the hours of manpower costs employed.

AI Predictions and Forecasts

AI is capable of predicting trends and customer behavior by analyzing data patterns. Uses for AI are advancing rapidly. For example, chatbots can now predict the emotional state of a customer when speaking to them over the phone, detecting whether they're angry, satisfied, or happy by analyzing tone. This advance makes understanding customer needs much faster, providing lessons for future growth.

Predictive analytics can help brands anticipate market changes, then create effective marketing strategies in response. Companies can reach audiences faster and better, because their messages have been tailored with the help of AI analytics to create a human touchpoint.

AI's use can be expanded to identify potential new products, or even different services customers may desire (yet the company may not have considered). Integrating AI creates more room for other vital ways to humanize brands. The biggest advantage is content generation, ranging from writing to creating content and product descriptions, generating basic articles, or writing reports that internal teams no longer need to waste their time on. By focusing on these more robotic elements of marketing, AI frees up teams to tackle more creative projects.

AI can also help brands maintain a consistent presence on digital platforms without requiring too many people or resources. For example, images, videos, and social media captions can be handled by AI then reviewed by humans, leading to higher productivity and lower costs. This boosts efficiency in operations by automating tasks and perhaps even improving supply chain management by predicting demand patterns.

As integration of AI can be applied to multiple levels of a company, it's the ideal way to keep ahead of the competition. AI should not be feared, therefore, but rather used to create better, more customer-focused branding.

TAKEAWAYS

The role of brands extends beyond mere transactions in this digital evolution, as they become facilitators of community, connection, and shared experiences. The journey ahead is about reimagining the possibilities of digital engagement, ensuring that every digital handshake, every online interaction, carries the warmth and sincerity of a human touch.

Look inside yourself and reflect on the journey of self-discovery while uncovering authentic stories. This meaningful content naturally leads us to the next pivotal step: creating effective strategies for fine-tuning the message on digital media. The raw, personal narratives we've identified and embraced must now be skillfully shaped and adapted to resonate across the vast digital landscape. We will take these deeply personal and authentic stories and tailor them for maximum impact on various digital platforms. We will explore the nuances of digital storytelling, from selecting the right channels to optimizing content for different digital environments. The ideal goal is to develop a comprehensive strategy that presents our stories authentically and ensures they reach and engage our intended audience effectively, making every share, like, and comment a testament to the power of genuine human connection in the Digital Age.

CHAPTER 9

LEVERAGING USER-GENERATED CONTENT

Authentic Application

We aren't living in a silo. We're humans, wired to be constantly connected and in communication with others. This is the era of user-generated content. It's not about turning customers into consumers—it's about turning them into *storytellers*.

User-generated content asks customers and consumers to engage with you via their own organic content. To do this, you could invite them to participate in a competition or connect with your company by posting a video while they're using or experiencing the brand.

Many brands are actually promoting user-generated content, because it's very authentic. You let your customers and consumers speak for you, not the other way around. This has proven to be extremely useful in building connections and heightening credibility.

User-generated content is cheaper, more organic, and most of all, authentic. In addition, it creates higher brand visibility because most users who generate content are influencers, with a wider reach and more intense engagement with their followers. Brands now go for this type of content creation to maximize their reach, impact, and results—all with minimal impact on the bottom line.

It's a win-win situation. It hits all the buttons.

CUSTOMERS ARE CO-CREATORS

The Digital Age demands more from brands and individuals than mere presence; it requires active, meaningful engagement that fosters two-way communication.

We are in a transformative era where the line between consumers and brand storytellers blurs. By the end of this chapter, you will be equipped with the knowledge and tools to turn your customers into active participants in your brand's narrative. This isn't merely about viewing customers as end-users but recognizing them as co-creators, whose experiences, insights, and contributions can enrich your brand's story and deepen its connection with the wider audience.

In a digital landscape where customer voices have the power to significantly influence brand perception, mastering the art of user-generated content becomes essential.

When a customer sees content created by someone just like them, the message no longer feels like a sales pitch; it becomes a recommendation from a trusted friend.

Have you ever stumbled upon a piece of content online that instantly made you feel connected to a brand, perhaps even before you'd ever purchased their product or service? This connection is often sparked by user-generated content (UGC)—real stories, photos, and reviews shared by real users. When it comes to learning about leveraging UGC in your own digital strategy, the answer lies in the power of authenticity and community.

The Process to Create User-Generated Content

The best way is to start by creating campaigns which request engagement. For example, you could run a campaign for a community of residents in a neighborhood, featuring an appealing landscape with many picture-perfect moments. With this campaign, the brand asks residents to use the amenities in the community and take a picture or video of themselves doing so, while speaking of their experience.

So, if a consumer bought a new garment or product, they could share their experience and tag the brand. The people creating this digital content don't even have to be influencers; they can be regular customers. The brand could even offer a gift to entice more people—for example, the people posting the first 10 images will receive a free gift. That way, a call to action is securely linked to the wider campaign.

So, what's in it for the user? Well, they're gaining more followers, a reward, or an acknowledgement. By sharing videos or pictures while being in the vicinity of a particular brand, the customer creates a positive association.

These increasing levels of engagement, supported by testimonials, steadily expand your brand's visibility while increasing your customer base. Curious people would want to visit the locations depicted, or even buy the product to try out the brand for themselves.

If the brand is an influencer, they need to pick and choose their videos carefully—after all, who do you want to have your brand linked with? It needs to be someone who stands for the same values, principles, and messaging, rather than anyone who could affect the brand negatively.

Here's why this information is crucial for anyone looking to elevate their brand in the Digital Age:

- Authenticity: UGC is perceived as more genuine than brand-created content. A study by Jose Angelo Gallegos at Tint found that 92% of consumers trust organic, user-generated content more than they trust traditional advertising. This authenticity can significantly enhance your brand's credibility and relatability.
- Engagement: Content created by users tends to receive higher engagement rates. It invites conversation and interaction, not just passive consumption. This interactive nature of UGC can lead to increased brand visibility and engagement on social media platforms.
- Conversion: Leveraging UGC can lead to higher conversion rates. According to a 2023 *Power Reviews* study, when users interact with UGC, they 'convert at a rate that's 102.4% higher than average.' By showcasing real people using your product or service, potential customers can more easily envision themselves doing the same, which can drive purchasing decisions.

CAMPAIGN METRICS

Brand ambassadorship and brand-integrated campaigns with influencers and public figures are also quite common. When taking the first steps to associating your brand with a famous person ... choose wisely. If this isn't done, a brand could pay a lot of money and invest extensive effort to associate with a chosen influencer without ever seeing the ROI (or even knowing what a 'ROI' is)!

There needs to be a measurable impact to choosing someone to represent you. Remember, it's not just about brand awareness; it's also about generating a return on your investment. What *is* the return on investment you're seeking? How will you calculate or measure it?

A well-constructed campaign encourages customers to respond to a call to action, share their experiences, and interact with customers while talking about the brand. That approach maintains authenticity, all while using diverse marketing channels to amplify customer advocacy. And remember, each one of these actions must be *measurable*.

Here are several specific tools and strategies to achieve this symbiotic relationship, ensuring mutual growth and loyalty.

1. Listening to Consumer Voices

Tool: Social Listening Platforms

- Description: Tools like Brandwatch or Hootsuite Insights allow brands to monitor mentions, hashtags, and conversations related to their products or services across various social media platforms.
- Application: Use these platforms to gather insights about what your audience is saying about your brand. Look for common themes, questions, or concerns that arise and address them directly in your content and offerings.
- Impact: By showing that you're actively listening and responding to your audience, you deepen their trust and loyalty. Their input can guide product development, content creation, and customer service improvements.

2. Aligning with Audience Ideals and Values

Tool: Audience Segmentation Software

- Description: Tools like HubSpot or Salesforce provide detailed analytics on your audience, allowing for precise segmentation based on interests, behaviors, and demographics.
- Application: Leverage this data to tailor your messaging and campaigns to reflect the values and interests of your segments. For example, if sustainability is a recurring theme, highlight eco-friendly aspects of your products or initiatives.
- Impact: Tailored messaging that resonates with your audience's values significantly enhances brand loyalty. It signals to consumers that your brand not only understands their concerns but also shares their ideals.

3. Showcasing User-Generated Content (UGC)

Tool: UGC Platforms like TINT or Yotpo

- Description: These platforms facilitate the collection, curation, and display of user-generated content from social media and other sources.
- Application: Encourage your audience to share their experiences with your brand using a specific hashtag. Curate this content and feature it prominently on your website, social media, and other marketing channels.
- Impact: Showcasing UGC serves as social proof, leveraging the credibility of peer recommendations. It visually demonstrates your product in action, enhancing trust and persuading new customers.

4. Creating Engagement Through Interaction

Tool: Interactive Content Creation Tools like Outgrow or Apester

- Description: These tools enable the creation of quizzes, polls, and interactive infographics that can increase engagement and collect valuable audience insights.
- Application: Develop interactive content that aligns with your audience's interests or challenges. Use the collected data to further personalize your marketing efforts.
- Impact: Interactive content not only captures attention but also encourages active participation, creating a more immersive brand experience. It's a powerful way to collect data while keeping your audience engaged.

5. Enhancing Brand Credibility and Recognition

Tool: Influencer Collaboration Platforms like AspireIQ or CreatorIQ

- Description: These platforms connect brands with influencers whose followers align with the brand's target audience.
- Application: Partner with influencers who share your brand's values and have a loyal following. Collaborate on content that highlights your products in a way that feels authentic and relatable.
- Impact: Influencer collaborations extend your brand's reach, leveraging the influencer's credibility to enhance your own. Authentic endorsements can significantly boost brand recognition and consumer trust.

By employing these tools and strategies, brands can foster a meaningful connection with their audience, ensuring that their marketing efforts resonate with consumer ideals and values. This approach amplifies brand visibility and credibility. It also cultivates a loyal community of consumers who feel seen, heard, and valued, achieving a true win-win scenario.

Case Study 1: TechStars, a SaaS Company

Background:

TechStars is a Software as a Service (SaaS) company providing project management solutions. Despite having a robust product, TechStars struggled with high customer acquisition costs and low conversion rates on their website.

Strategy:

TechStars decided to incorporate customer testimonials into their marketing strategy, focusing on stories that highlighted significant improvements in project efficiency and team collaboration among their users.

Implementation:

1. Collection: TechStars reached out to long-term customers, requesting testimonials that specifically addressed how the software had impacted their operations.

2. Showcase: The company created a dedicated 'Success Stories' section on their website, where they featured video testimonials, including detailed narratives of how customers achieved specific results using TechStars' solution.

3. Integration: Testimonials were also integrated into product pages, email marketing campaigns, and social media posts, with clear CTAs leading back to the success stories on their website.

Results:

- Within three months, TechStars saw a 40% increase in website engagement and a 25% increase in conversion rates.
- The 'Success Stories' section became one of the most visited pages on the website.
- Social media posts featuring customer testimonials received higher engagement rates compared to other content types.

Case Study 2: GreenThumb, an Organic Gardening Supply Brand

Background:

GreenThumb offers a range of organic gardening supplies but faced challenges in differentiating itself in a crowded market. The brand needed a way to authentically connect with its target audience of environmentally conscious gardeners.

Strategy:

GreenThumb launched a campaign encouraging customers to share their gardening success stories and the impact of using organic products on their gardens' health and yield.

Implementation:

1. User-Generated Content (UGC) Campaign: Customers were encouraged to share their stories and photos on social media using the hashtag #GreenThumbSuccess, with the incentive of being featured on GreenThumb's platforms.

2. Curated Showcase: The most compelling stories were featured on GreenThumb's website and social media channels, including detailed 'before and after' transformations.

3. Engagement: GreenThumb actively engaged with all participants, thanking them for their submissions and commenting on posts, fostering a sense of community.

Results:

- The campaign generated a significant amount of UGC, with over 1,000 tagged posts within the first two months.
- GreenThumb experienced a 35% increase in social media followers and a 20% uptick in direct sales attributed to the campaign.

- Customer testimonials served as powerful social proof, enhancing GreenThumb's credibility and authentic connection with its audience.

These case studies from TechStars and GreenThumb illustrate the versatility and effectiveness of customer testimonials across different industries. By strategically integrating testimonials into their marketing efforts, both companies were able to enhance their brand credibility, engage more deeply with their audience, and achieve tangible improvements in their marketing metrics. These examples underscore the power of authentic customer voices in shaping brand perceptions and driving business success.

STORYTELLING CASE STUDIES

1. IKEA: Enhancing Lives Through Design

Background: IKEA, the world-renowned furniture and home goods company, has masterfully utilized storytelling to position itself not just as a retailer but a brand committed to improving everyday lives through thoughtful, sustainable design. Their approach to marketing goes beyond showcasing products, focusing instead on how their solutions fit into the personal narratives of customers' lives.

Impactful Storytelling:

- 'The Wonderful Everyday' Campaign: IKEA's campaigns often feature real-life stories that highlight how their products can transform mundane daily routines into something wonderful. By focusing on the emotional impact of their designs on family life, personal space, and even sustainability efforts, IKEA crafts a narrative that resonates with a broad audience.

- Sustainability Narratives: IKEA has committed to becoming a fully circular and climate-positive business by 2030. Through storytelling, they share their journey towards this goal, including sustainable product lines and initiatives that encourage customers to live more sustainably. These stories not only inform but also inspire customers to be part of the sustainability solution.

Outcome: IKEA has successfully cultivated a global community of customers who see IKEA not just as a store but as a source of inspiration for a better, more sustainable way of living. Their storytelling approach has reinforced the brand's reputation for innovation, quality, and social responsibility, making IKEA a beloved part of many homes around the world.

2. Airbnb: Fostering Connection Through Shared Experiences

Background: Airbnb, a global online marketplace for lodging and tourism experiences, leverages storytelling to transform how people perceive travel. The brand emphasizes the unique experiences and personal connections made through its service, distinguishing itself in the hospitality industry.

Impactful Storytelling:

- 'Belong Anywhere' Campaign: Airbnb uses real stories from hosts and travelers to illustrate the concept of belonging anywhere. By sharing these personal narratives, they highlight the diverse, authentic experiences available through Airbnb, from staying in unique homes to immersive local activities.

- User-Generated Content: Encouraging guests and hosts to share their stories on social media, Airbnb's platform becomes a tapestry of personal travel experiences, showcasing the brand's impact on real people's lives. These examples of user-generated content serve as authentic testimonials to the enriching experiences Airbnb offers.

Outcome: Airbnb has successfully positioned itself as more than a booking platform; it's a community that connects people across the globe through shared spaces and experiences. Their emphasis on storytelling has helped foster a sense of belonging and community, appealing to travelers seeking authentic, personal travel experiences.

IKEA and Airbnb showcase the power of storytelling in creating deep, meaningful connections with audiences worldwide. Through narratives that emphasize life-enhancing designs and unique travel experiences, both brands have not only solidified their market positions but also inspired a loyal following that values their contributions to improving lifestyles and fostering global connections.

Get Started

Now that we've explored the impactful role of user-generated content (UGC) in fostering brand advocacy, it's time to put these insights into action. Here's what you should consider and implement as your next steps:

1. Encourage Customer Participation: Develop creative and engaging strategies that motivate your customers to share their experiences and stories. This could involve social media challenges, hashtag campaigns, or contests that invite users to post content related to how they use your product or service in their daily lives.

2. Implement Moderation Practices: While embracing UGC, it's crucial to establish moderation practices that ensure the content shared aligns with your brand values and maintains authenticity. Create clear guidelines for submission, and consider tools or dedicated team members to review and approve content before it's showcased.

3. Showcase Across Marketing Channels: Leverage a variety of marketing channels to showcase user-generated content. From featuring customer stories on your website to sharing UGC on social media platforms and incorporating it into email marketing campaigns, diversifying your approach can significantly amplify the reach and impact of customer advocacy.

4. Create Engaging Campaigns: Craft campaigns that highlight user-generated content and reinforce the sense of community among your customers. Tailor these campaigns to encourage ongoing participation and dialogue, ensuring that your brand remains a dynamic and interactive presence in their lives.

By following these steps, you'll be able to harness the power of user-generated content effectively, transforming satisfied customers into vocal brand advocates.

TAKEAWAYS

When brands actively feature customer content, it achieves two key outcomes: It validates the customer's contribution by making them feel valued and seen, and it demonstrates to the wider audience the real-world application and satisfaction derived from the brand's offerings. This recognition fosters a deeper connection between the brand and its customers, encouraging them to become more vocal and enthusiastic advocates. They are likely to share their positive experiences not only with their immediate circle but also with a broader audience through social media, forums, and word of mouth.

Furthermore, leveraging UGC facilitates a dynamic dialogue between the brand and its community, fostering a sense of belonging and loyalty among customers. It transforms passive consumers into active participants in the brand's narrative, creating a vibrant community of supporters who are eager to share their stories and experiences. This chapter underscores the value of amplifying user-generated content as a means to not only bolster brand visibility but also to cultivate a loyal, engaged customer base that is instrumental in driving brand growth and advocacy.

In an era where consumers are increasingly savvy and demand authenticity from the brands they support, the value of trust cannot be overstated. The next chapter explores how maintaining transparency and upholding trust are not merely ethical choices but strategic imperatives that drive long-term loyalty and sustainable success.

CHAPTER 10

TRUST AND TRANSPARENCY

Building Connections with Credibility

Trust is a key element that creates long-term loyalty and builds connections with credibility.

At times, when some brands are attempting to humanize themselves, they'll lie to sell a product.

They'll do that because they want to make themselves look better than the competition. They pretend to be someone that they're not in order to gain followers, reach, or engagement on social media.

Unfortunately, this doesn't work in the long term.

Let's go by the school of thought that 'You can fool some of the people some of the time, but you can't fool everybody all of the time.'

Therefore, establishing trust through open communication and transparency is very important for long-term credibility.

This chapter is about incorporating ethical practices and social responsibility into your brand strategies. That's because everybody's now looking to see how brands contribute to community development, add to their society, and make a difference.

As much as the company makes profit, they must also give back— so it's profit *and* planet. Long-term trust-building isn't just about the bottom line; it's also about how you give back to your society.

Remembering this helps a brand to stand out from the crowd, differentiating it from competitors by being perceived as responsible and sustainable. Even more importantly, it gives the brand an edge.

IMPORTANCE OF TRUST FOR LONG-TERM SUSTAINABILITY

Have you ever stood before a vast sea of products, wondering which to choose? Think about the last time you made a purchase decision. Was it the brand story or the product's impact on the environment that influenced you? In today's market, filled with endless options, it's not just the quality or price that sets a product apart—it's the commitment to sustainability. Reflect on this: How does choosing a sustainable product not only benefit you, but also contribute to a larger global impact? This question opens the door to understanding why embracing sustainability in the market is not just important—it's essential.

I remember walking through a local farmers' market, drawn to a stall with the most vibrant fresh produce. The farmer shared his story of sustainable farming practices, explaining how every choice he made was rooted in respect for the land and the future. This personal connection transformed my shopping habits. It wasn't just about the freshness of the produce but also the story behind it, the impact of my choices on the environment, and the legacy we leave for future generations. This story exemplifies why understanding and choosing sustainability in the market matters. It's about seeing beyond the immediate, recognizing our role in a larger ecosystem, and making choices that support it.

Recent studies have shown that 73% of global consumers are willing to change their consumption habits to reduce environmental impact. Furthermore, companies that lead in sustainability practices see a 15% increase in sales on average. This evidence highlights a clear trend: Sustainability is not just a buzzword; it's a business imperative. Consumers are increasingly making choices based on a company's environmental impact, driving a significant shift in the market. This shift is creating opportunities for businesses to stand out from the crowd, setting a new standard in consumer expectations. Understanding this trend and integrating sustainability into business practices is crucial for differentiation and long-term success in the competitive market landscape.

Through these approaches, we explore the importance of sustainability in the market. Whether it's a moment of reflection, a personal connection, or the undeniable evidence of changing consumer preferences, the message is clear: Sustainability is the key to standing out, differentiating from competitors, and ensuring long-term success in today's market.

Building Connections With Credibility: A Story of Trust and Transparency

Navigating the corporate landscape demands a strategic blend of innovation, performance, and, most critically, a foundation of trust and transparency. This narrative is vividly illustrated in the journey of TechGlobal Solutions, a leading corporate entity that redefined industry standards through its unwavering commitment to ethical practices and client engagement.

TechGlobal Solutions, with its extensive portfolio in cutting-edge corporate solutions, embarked on an ambitious initiative to integrate ethical governance and transparency into its core operational ethos. Recognizing the growing demand for corporate accountability, the company set out to foster trust and transparency not as mere buzzwords but as pillars of its corporate identity.

Enhancing Client Engagement Through Transparency

TechGlobal initiated its transformation by instituting a policy of radical transparency with its clients. This involved openly sharing information on operational practices, compliance standards, and ethical governance. The company went a step further by implementing a real-time tracking system for clients, offering unprecedented access to the lifecycle of services and products, from development to delivery. This level of openness was groundbreaking, positioning TechGlobal as a trailblazer in corporate transparency.

Cultivating Trust Through Ethical Leadership

Trust was meticulously cultivated through the company's consistent demonstration of ethical leadership and accountability. When faced with a service failure that impacted several clients, TechGlobal's response was swift and transparent. The company rectified the issue at no additional cost to the clients and initiated a comprehensive review of its operations, leading to significant improvements in service delivery. This response underscored TechGlobal's commitment to its ethical standards and solidified client trust.

Fostering Connections With Credibility

Beyond transparency and ethical governance, TechGlobal sought to actively involve its clients in shaping the future of its services. The company established a Client Innovation Council, a forum where clients could voice challenges, suggest innovations, and directly influence service enhancements. This initiative not only spurred innovation but also created a sense of partnership between TechGlobal and its clients, deepening their connection through shared goals and mutual respect.

Impact and Industry Recognition

The outcomes of TechGlobal's strategy were transformative. The company not only saw an uptick in client retention and satisfaction but also gained recognition as a leader in corporate responsibility. TechGlobal's approach attracted positive media attention and led to several accolades for ethical business practices and innovation in client engagement.

A Corporate Model for the Future

TechGlobal Solutions' journey offers a compelling blueprint for how corporations can navigate the demands of the modern business environment. By prioritizing transparency, upholding ethical standards, and fostering collaborative client relationships, companies can create a competitive edge that is built on the solid foundation of trust and credibility. TechGlobal's story serves as a powerful reminder that in the world of corporate business, the path to success is increasingly defined by the integrity of one's practices and the strength of one's commitments to clients.

TechGlobal Solutions exemplifies the critical role of trust and transparency in building and maintaining strong corporate relationships. This narrative not only highlights the strategic importance of ethical practices but also illuminates the path for businesses seeking to cultivate a reputation for credibility and integrity in a complex corporate landscape.

Now, let's turn our attention to a very different sector, where cut-throat profit margins and ruthless competition tend to squeeze out those with good intentions. We'll touch on several companies who are managing to offer a hopeful counterpoint to the industry's reputation for exploitation.

THE CHALLENGES FACING URBAN CLOTH RETAILERS

Today's urban cloth retailers face a rapidly evolving landscape, marked by intense competition and shifting consumer preferences. The rise of fast fashion has intensified pressures to produce trendy, affordable clothes at a breakneck pace, often at the expense of quality and sustainability. However, this model is increasingly being challenged by a growing demand for transparency and ethical responsibility. Modern consumers, especially younger generations, expect brands to not only deliver style and affordability but also to be socially and environmentally conscious. In this context, urban retailers must navigate a delicate balance—maintaining profitability while aligning their business practices with the ethical and sustainable values of their audience.

While the fashion sector is especially challenging for ethically oriented companies, given its history of worker exploitation and environmental damage, several have taken the lead by creating desirable products while adhering to noble principles. As the following examples show, fashion need not be incompatible with a moral purpose. By looking at several notable campaigns, we'll pinpoint how it's possible to take the lead in a particularly challenging retail environment.

Case Studies of Ethical Practices and Storytelling in Urban Clothing Retail

1. The Giving Movement: Activism-Driven Storytelling

The Giving Movement is not just a brand—it's a clear example of how post-COVID ventures can humanize their identity while balancing profit and social impact. By focusing on purpose-driven values, it deeply connects with a more conscious consumer base that seeks authenticity and meaningful engagement. The brand's communication doesn't merely emphasize its sustainable materials or charitable donations; it brings forward the stories behind those choices, making the brand feel more personal and relatable.

Humanizing brands, especially in the post-pandemic era, is about showing that businesses can care about more than just profits. The Giving Movement does this by embodying its values in every touchpoint. Whether it's showcasing the artisans and workers involved in production, highlighting the real-world impact of the charitable donations, or engaging directly with its audience on social media to discuss sustainability and giving back, the brand ensures that every interaction feels authentic and human.

This approach transforms The Giving Movement into more than just a clothing brand. It becomes a movement that consumers want to be part of, fostering a community where customers feel like their purchases have a direct positive impact. By humanizing its communication, the brand doesn't just sell products; it sells a mission, a story, and a sense of belonging to something bigger than fashion—an idea that resonates deeply in a post-pandemic world where authenticity and purpose drive consumer decisions.

This model can serve as a blueprint for other brands looking to create an emotional connection with their audience, proving that humanizing a brand can elevate both profit and impact.

2. Everlane: Radical Transparency

- Ethical Practices: Everlane has made transparency a cornerstone of its brand. They reveal the true cost of making their clothes, breaking down materials, labor, and transport costs to the consumer.
- Campaign Example: Their 'Know Your Factories' initiative offers insight into their production process by featuring videos and profiles of factory workers, shining a light on ethical labor practices.
- Humanizing Element: By sharing stories of the people behind the clothes and how they source materials, Everlane creates a direct connection between the consumer and the makers. Their ethical approach builds trust, making the customer feel part of a movement toward more responsible consumption.

3. H&M: Sustainable Collection and Greenwashing Challenges

- Ethical Practices: H&M's Conscious Collection is a move toward more sustainable fashion, featuring items made from organic and recycled materials. They are investing in circular fashion technology and have set ambitious sustainability goals.
- Campaign Example: Their storytelling often focuses on the future of fashion being sustainable, with campaigns including 'Close the Loop' encouraging people to recycle their old clothes in exchange for vouchers.
- Humanizing Element: Although H&M is sometimes accused of greenwashing, they are taking steps to be more transparent about their sustainability journey. Highlighting real-life sustainability efforts (like customer recycling programs) in their campaigns humanizes their brand, showing they are trying to improve.

4. TOMS: The One-for-One Model and Beyond

- Ethical Practices: TOMS became famous for its one-for-one model, where every purchase of their shoes leads to a pair being donated to someone in need.
- Campaign Example: TOMS has continuously told emotional stories of the impact their shoes have had on disadvantaged communities worldwide. Their campaigns focus on the people who benefit from their donations, making it personal and relatable.
- Humanizing Element: TOMS' humanized brand comes from its direct social impact. Their campaigns show the real faces of those helped, which not only builds emotional ties with consumers but also strengthens the company's mission-driven identity.

Responsible Marketing and Engaging Storytelling

5. Nike: Social Activism in Marketing

- Ethical Practices: Nike's approach to social activism, particularly through athletes and movements like Black Lives Matter, has set them apart as a brand willing to take risks.
- Campaign Example: The 'Dream Crazy' campaign, featuring Colin Kaepernick, took a bold stance on social justice issues. While it was a story about dreaming big, it also emphasized Nike's support of individual rights and activism.
- Humanizing Element: By aligning themselves with a controversial cause, Nike wasn't just marketing shoes—they were selling the values of justice and empowerment. Their commitment to telling stories about athletes who defy the odds adds a personal touch to their high-performance image.

These urban cloth retailers are now in a position where ethical practices, when combined with authentic storytelling, can turn consumers into loyal advocates for their brands.

Each of these examples shows how ethical marketing and storytelling not only engage the audience but also transform brands into meaningful, purpose-driven entities.

REPUTATION MANAGEMENT

Reputation serves as the foundation upon which trust is built between consumers and brands. It's not merely about the quality of products or services but also about the integrity, reliability, and ethical standards a company upholds. Here's how reputation plays a crucial role in building trust.

If there's a crisis in the market or a reputational problem with a brand, customer loyalty will remain high if the brand has already done much for the community by acting with a sense of social responsibility. Such a brand will be able to navigate through these challenges and reputational hazards more smoothly than one that's never done anything for other people and only cares about profit. In other words, there's a cushion. The brand has some valuable goodwill to fall back on, without appearing PR-hungry.

When some companies face issues or crises, they come out saying, 'Oh, but we've done *this*. We've done *that*.' Yet even if they have done a lot for the community in the past, people won't believe them because they weren't vocal about it until it was too late. Instead, they'll think it was all a PR stunt.

Now, consider the alternative. If trust-building has been part of a company's messaging, action plan, and core principles for many years, and they've created a positive impact with reportable, transparent, and credible results, people will tend to treat the crisis as a one-off.

This is most unlike the too-common situation that unfolds when an oil and gas company has an oil spill in the ocean, for example. It's obvious that they've never cared about protecting marine life, yet they still come out saying, 'We're committed to ...'

What have they done? Nothing! They're just offering lip service. As part of any company's crisis management, the brand's representatives need to be proactive, not reactive. They need to forecast when a crisis might hit, even if it's a decade from now.

Consistent Messaging

Consistency across quality, service, and messaging is a cornerstone of brand reliability and customer loyalty, especially in the sustainability sector. This consistency forms a cohesive brand experience that reinforces trust and differentiates a company from its competitors.

All successful brands must make sure they hire the right Chief Communications Officer. Even though this is a crucial position, many companies shy away from investing in an extensive communications team. Communication is the backbone of the company, providing the company with the right exposure, messaging, and narrative.

When disaster strikes, the brand won't know what to do without a crack communications team. While it's okay to outsource your PR agency, the brand also needs a smart and efficient Communications Officer with a cool head to steer the mothership in tough times. PR agencies can't do this, because they're external. Instead, the brand will need a visionary insider who understands the company's vision, as well as its ins and outs. They must have access to confidential information, so that they can tell who the most important people to reach are when the ship's in trouble.

Unfortunately, though, many companies cut their communications staff first when they have to cut costs.

A company which doesn't recognize the value of a Communications Officer is like one without a finance, legal, or HR team. Communication is the main pillar of success, so how can you ignore the importance of internal and external communications?

It's become increasingly important to have a team which lives and breathes the brand, while constantly thinking, 'What's next?'. The brand always has to be up and about, scoping out what's new in the market and how benchmarks have evolved. How can they stay ahead of the curve? How can they be edgy? How can they communicate differently about their people to the stakeholders, investors, and customers? How can they make the brand different and non-traditional? How can they elevate the brand? How can they support the Marketing team, the Branding team, and the Production team in order to communicate properly?

This is all part of the Communications team's responsibility, enabling the company to build trust by publicizing their integrity, authenticity, and reputation while maintaining consistency. Basically, a great Communications team needs to convincingly show that the product or service leads with purpose and creates impact.

The Ultimate Purpose

A given company's ultimate purpose involves embedding deep-rooted corporate values, exceptional customer service, and a steadfast reputation in the tapestry of modern business operations. These foundational elements are beneficial practices and essential strategies for fostering long-term trust and loyalty both within and outside the organization.

Corporate Values: Establishing clear, actionable corporate values is the cornerstone of any business aiming for sustainability and ethical operation. These values act as a guiding star, influencing decisions, shaping company culture, and ensuring that every action taken aligns with the broader mission of social and environmental responsibility.

Customer Service: Exceptional customer service transcends the traditional boundaries of transactional interactions, evolving into a powerful tool for building enduring trust and rapport. By treating every customer interaction as an opportunity to demonstrate the company's commitment to its values and ethics, businesses can cultivate a loyal customer base that values integrity and authenticity.

Reputation: A solid reputation, built on the pillars of transparency, consistency, and accountability, becomes the ultimate currency in the modern market. It's a *reflection* of a company's commitment to its values, the quality of its customer service, and its ability to consistently deliver on promises. A stellar reputation not only attracts customers but also inspires confidence among stakeholders, partners, and employees.

In summary, the integration of corporate values, unparalleled customer service, and a robust reputation is not just a strategy for business success; it's a blueprint for building meaningful, trust-based relationships in today's competitive and ever-evolving marketplace.

Now It's Your Turn

Examine Your Values: Start by taking a comprehensive look at your organization's values. This includes not just the corporate and organizational values but also the brand and personal values of the leaders within. Assess whether these values are clearly defined, communicated, and understood across all levels of your organization. It's crucial that these values are not just words on a website or a poster on a wall, but principles that guide decision-making, behavior, and business practices.

Evaluate Alignment: Once you've clarified your values, the next step is to evaluate their alignment with your products or services. Ask yourself whether your offerings genuinely reflect your values. Are you practicing what you preach? For instance, if sustainability is a core value, does your product's lifecycle—from sourcing to disposal—uphold this principle? This alignment is critical not just for internal consistency but for building credibility and trust with your customers.

Take Action: Identify areas where your values and your business practices may not fully align and develop a plan to address these gaps. This might involve revising policies, rethinking supply chains, or enhancing customer service protocols to ensure that your values are lived and breathed within every aspect of your organization.

The journey towards aligning your values with your products or services is both challenging and rewarding. It requires introspection, honesty, and the willingness to make necessary changes. By undertaking this journey, you position your organization not just for success in the marketplace but as a leader in ethical and sustainable business practices. Let your next step be a commitment to aligning your values with your actions, thereby driving positive change within your organization and the communities you serve.

TAKEAWAYS

For this approach to succeed, people must believe that the company's commitment to transparency isn't a PR stunt. It has to be embedded in company strategy, both internally and externally.

That means the company must have clear values, enforced from the top down. Everyone pursues the same vision, making sure the company's reputation is maintained.

This leads us to understanding the alchemy of personalized brand experiences. In a world full of virtually limitless choice, consumers seek more than products; they seek meaningful experiences as well. This new way of marketing your company is about far more than the product or service alone. Instead, it's about the personalized customer service you provide.

CHAPTER 11

TAILORING BRAND EXPERIENCES

The Alchemy of Personalization

Imagine a world where every brand interaction feels like it was crafted just for you. Where your preferences, needs, and desires are not just recognized but anticipated. This is not a distant future or a marketer's daydream—it's the emerging reality of personalized brand experiences. How does this shift affect your connection with the brands you love? Let's explore the magic behind making every customer feel like the *only* customer.

Making all customers feel as if the brand is talking to them, so the message *isn't* one size fits all, is a unique skill. Yet the brand can only achieve this if they understand their customers' demography, needs, style, culture, and even heritage. These factors play a huge role in personalizing a brand experience.

This special form of communication between brand and customer requires the ability to see each person as an individual, not a sales target. By doing this sincerely, brands build relationships with their clients.

Customer-centric experiences make individuals feel special. Even if the message has been sent out to the general public, each person feels as if it's coming directly from the brand. For this reason, each message must be crafted to reflect a person's individual use of language and specific needs.

For brands like Nescafé, Lipton, and Colgate, creating content that resonates with different sectors—such as real estate and food & beverage (F&B)—requires a strategic blend of storytelling, industry insights, and engaging support materials. This approach not only informs and entertains the audience but also subtly reinforces the brand's value proposition. Discover how content can be crafted for these brands, providing examples and suggesting supporting materials to enhance the narrative.

MASTERING PERSONALIZED CUSTOMER SERVICE: A STEP-BY-STEP GUIDE

To truly excel in providing personalized customer service, it's essential to understand your audience and recognize that not all customers are the same. Here's a practical guide to achieving this, broken down into clear steps:

1. Segment Your Customers

The first step is to categorize your customers into distinct segments based on common characteristics, such as demographics, purchasing behaviors, and preferences. This process enables you to understand the diverse needs and expectations of different customer groups.

How to Do It: Utilize your customer database to analyze purchasing patterns, feedback, and engagement levels. Tools like CRM software can automate this process, providing insights into customer behaviors and preferences.

2. Create Detailed Customer Personas

Once you've segmented your customers, the next step is to develop detailed personas for each segment. A persona is a semi-fictional character that represents a significant portion of your audience, based on your research and data analysis.

How to Do It: Gather information from a variety of sources including sales data, customer surveys, and social media analytics. Each persona should include demographic details, interests, pain points, and buying motivations to guide personalized interactions.

3. Implement a Customer Recognition System

Recognizing your customers on an individual level is crucial for personalized service. This means knowing their history with your brand, their preferences, and even their past concerns.

How to Do It: Use technology to your advantage by implementing systems that allow you to identify and greet customers by name, recall their last purchase or interaction, and tailor your communication based on their preferences.

4. Train Your Team on Personalization Techniques

Your team should understand the importance of personalization and be equipped with the skills to execute it effectively. This includes communication skills, empathy, and the ability to use customer data responsibly.

How to Do It: Conduct regular training sessions and workshops focusing on personalization strategies, use of customer data, and case studies of successful personalized customer service.

5. Measure and Adjust Your Strategies

Finally, it's important to track the effectiveness of your personalization efforts and make adjustments as needed. This involves measuring customer satisfaction, loyalty, and feedback related to personalized experiences.

How to Do It: Use surveys, feedback forms, and metrics such as Net Promoter Score (NPS) to gauge customer responses. Analyze this data to identify areas for improvement and refine your personalization strategies accordingly.

By following these steps and focusing on recognizing the unique needs and preferences of each customer, you can elevate your customer service from basic to exceptional, fostering stronger relationships and building a loyal customer base.

Here are some great examples:

Nescafé: Energizing the Real Estate Sector

Visuals and Supporting Material: An infographic highlighting the benefits of coffee in enhancing workplace productivity and creativity sets the stage. Additionally, a step-by-step guide or video tutorial on integrating Nescafé coffee stations in office spaces could serve as practical advice for real estate developers and companies.

Content Example: Imagine a scenario where a forward-thinking real estate developer partners with Nescafé to install stylish modern coffee stations in new office complexes. This initiative, aimed at boosting worker satisfaction and productivity, becomes a major selling point. Through interviews with employees who have experienced a boost in their daily performance and overall job satisfaction thanks to the readily available Nescafé coffee, the story comes to life. This narrative not only showcases the developer's innovative approach but also emphasizes Nescafé's role in enhancing workplace environments.

Supporting Material: Offer a downloadable guide on creating efficient and inviting office spaces, emphasizing the role of coffee in fostering a positive work environment. Include links to Nescafé products and equipment tailored for office use.

Lipton: Refreshing Innovations in F&B

Visuals and Supporting Material: Create a vibrant chart comparing the popularity of different Lipton teas, alongside a visual recipe book for innovative tea-based drinks and dishes.

Content Example: Highlight the story of an F&B entrepreneur who revamps their menu to include a variety of dishes and beverages infused with Lipton teas. This menu innovation leads to a surge in popularity, attracting a diverse clientele eager to try these unique offerings. The entrepreneur shares insights into the creative process and the positive impact on their business, underscoring Lipton's versatility and appeal in culinary creations.

Supporting Material: A template for F&B businesses to experiment with tea-infused recipes, coupled with blog articles on the health benefits of incorporating tea into one's diet, linking back to Lipton's product range.

Colgate: Smiles Across Sectors

Visuals and Supporting Material: A gallery showcasing before and after results of using Colgate products for dental health, alongside diagrams for designing bathroom spaces with Colgate stations in residential properties.

Content Example: In the real estate sector, an innovative property management company includes Colgate oral care kits in their welcome packages for new tenants, enhancing tenant satisfaction and wellbeing. Meanwhile, in the F&B industry, a high-end restaurant partners with Colgate to offer guests complimentary post-meal oral care kits, elevating the dining experience and emphasizing the importance of dental health.

Supporting Material: Checklists for real estate agents on creating welcoming and thoughtful spaces for tenants, and guides for F&B owners and thoroughly incorporating wellness practices into their establishments, featuring Colgate dental care products.

Through these detailed examples and supporting materials, the content not only promotes Nescafé, Lipton, and Colgate but also provides tangible value to the audience, bridging the gap between brand and consumer in a meaningful way.

BUILDING A PERSONALIZED RELATIONSHIP USING AI

AI now plays a huge role, with many of the new applications and technologies that have emerged helping to radically increase time efficiency by customizing the various processes in an organization. A task which may take a human hundreds of hours to complete could take AI 15 minutes.

After you have all of the content and brand assets in place, you can apply them in a way that develops the customer relationship by creating a personalized experience. These customers will spread positive word of mouth, resulting in a positive trend emerging. To do this, though, it's vital to know the customer in detail.

You'll have to start with a plan, discover your target audience, build a communication profile, and then address this audience (being sensitive to language, culture, and background).

For example, you wouldn't address a Chinese customer in exactly the same way as you'd address someone from Russia or India. Every culture and language is different, with many words and phrases lost in translation.

So, from a single letter all the way to a complete campaign, the brand has to create content specifically for each target language, combining the right words, messaging, and narratives with sensitivity to the target audience's specific context.

That's how household names like Nescafé and Lipton are built—famous names which experience generational growth.

For AI-driven personalization to succeed, brands must invest in sophisticated AI technology, ensure continuous learning and adaptation, balance AI automation with the human touch, prioritize customer privacy, and align personalization efforts with customer values. By addressing these conditions, brands can forge deeper, more meaningful connections with their customers, transcending the perception of customers as mere numbers.

GET STARTED: SWOT ANALYSIS

Strengths

Positive Customer Feedback: Identify patterns in positive feedback that highlight your brand's success in providing personalized service. This could include commendations on staff friendliness, responsiveness, or how well your team understands customer needs and preferences.

Brand Loyalty Indicators: Look for evidence of repeat business, referrals, or positive social media mentions as indicators of strong brand reputation and loyalty, which are direct outcomes of effective personalization.

Weaknesses

Negative Feedback and Complaints: Analyze customer complaints and negative reviews to identify common themes. These might relate to perceived indifference, lack of understanding of customer needs, or failures in recognizing returning customers.

Inconsistencies in Service: Identify any patterns of inconsistency in service delivery, such as varying levels of personalization across different channels or locations, which can dilute the overall effectiveness of your personalization efforts.

Opportunities

Leveraging Technology for Better Personalization: With the rise of AI and machine learning, there's significant opportunity to enhance personalization through better data analysis and predictive modeling, leading to more tailored customer experiences.

Expanding Personalization to New Channels: Explore opportunities to extend personalized interactions to new platforms or channels where your customers are active but your brand has not fully engaged, such as social media or messaging apps.

Threats

Competitive Pressure: Recognize that competitors may also be improving their personalization efforts, which can threaten to diminish the uniqueness of your brand's customer service experience.

Privacy Concerns: In an era where data privacy is paramount, there's a fine line between personalization and perceived invasion of privacy. Missteps in how personal data is used can lead to customer distrust and damage to brand reputation.

Conducting the Analysis

Gather Data: Use customer feedback tools, social media listening platforms, and direct customer surveys to collect comprehensive data on customer perceptions.

Analyze Feedback: Systematically categorize feedback to identify strengths, weaknesses, opportunities, and threats.

Develop Actionable Insights: Based on your SWOT analysis, identify specific actions to enhance strengths, address weaknesses, seize opportunities, and mitigate threats. This might include training staff on privacy practices, investing in new technologies for better data analysis, or creating more personalized marketing campaigns.

By understanding and addressing the challenges and opportunities identified through a SWOT analysis, your brand can enhance its reputation for personalized customer service, ultimately leading to a stronger connection with your customers and a competitive edge in the market.

TAKEAWAYS

All this emphasis on personalized marketing and the leveraging of data analytics naturally leads us to the vital component at the core of all these efforts: the human element. Understanding and implementing technology and strategies for personalization sets the stage, but it's the genuine connection and emotional resonance that truly transform customer experiences.

This segues perfectly to our next chapter, where we'll get into humanizing brands. We'll explore how brands can embody human traits, communicate authentically, and build relationships that transcend transactions, ensuring that every customer interaction feels personal, meaningful, and distinctly human.

CHAPTER 12

HUMANIZING BRANDS

Synergizing the Personal
and the Organizational

Authenticity isn't a fleeting concept; it's the foundation of impactful personal branding. We've already discussed storytelling, building credibility, and ensuring transparency. We've recognized the human dimension within organizations, and also that those within the organization, as brand ambassadors, should believe in the brand. Eventually, it's this additional human dimension within an organization that enhances personal branding.

A brand can't choose to *sometimes* be customer-centric, or authentic, or transparent, or trustworthy. As an entity with the power to change lives, a brand has a greater responsibility to maintain a consistency capable of lasting through the generations. Walking the talk requires investing in people who genuinely believe in the brand's culture, creating a domino effect which will humanize every aspect of the business.

PEOPLE CONNECTING PEOPLE

Reputation is a two-way street, so you want people to speak highly of your organization. Brands need to embody the process of leading by example, doing so with a sense of purpose and empathy. In this area, people are a brand's biggest asset.

Post-COVID, success has become more about brand advocacy. If a brand doesn't focus on retention, customers won't remain loyal to them in the long term.

If a brand persistently invests in people who stay around for a few months, then take their money and leave, this easily becomes a repetitive cycle without any sense of loyalty. Conversely, a brand can become human-centric if it makes customers feel as if they're part of an organization that cares about their staff, their community, and their customers. This type of empathetic culture is based on a human-centric approach. Staff will tend to stay on through the hardest times, not just the good times.

If this type of company is going through a financial or another type of crisis, its staff will tend to stay on board. They will become the brand's biggest ambassadors and champions, speaking highly of the brand regardless of everything else, because they feel an affiliation towards the company they work for.

That's why customer loyalty starts within the organization itself. All those working within it must have a sincere sense of affiliation towards the brand, consistently speaking of the association with a sense of pride.

That's how employees can invest in the growth of the organization from within. Whether you're a student, a C-suite leader, an athlete, a real estate agent, an author, a publisher, or any other occupation, personal branding is vital. It refers to how a person identifies themselves in the world, as well as whom they represent.

Many people are now realizing the paramount importance of personal branding. In one sense, every person's whole *personality* is a brand, because it's how they present themselves. The pillars of this personality are your values, which define what you stand for and whom you become. It's the way you communicate with and influence others in your life. If you're active on social media, your personal brand dictates how you share information and educate people about your industry, and how you're perceived during events or within the team.

You are a Brand

Mark Twain said, 'There are two very important days in your life. The first is the day you're born, and the second is the day you find out why.' I always believe that everybody is here on this planet for a reason. Everyone has something special that they came into this world to offer.

Some people live their lives without knowing what their purpose is, or they use their skills in the wrong ways. On the other hand, some people are lucky enough to know their purpose early on, and are then able to use this correctly.

So, if you know your purpose (your 'why'), take ownership of this, then start sharing it with the world. If you're in an influential role, this is crucial. If you're a teacher, you're influencing the younger generation; if you're an athlete, you're influencing others involved in your sport, many of whom will be inspired by you. Either way, you need to be a role model.

That means you need to rise to the occasion. You can't be in an influential position while simultaneously being careless and irresponsible. As Spider-Man says, 'With great power comes great responsibility.'

With everybody now sharing their lives on social media, it feels like every other person and their mothers are calling themselves 'influencers'.

You have to find your tribe, the people who are genuine, those who have a message and purpose.

Empower Hour, DBate Podcast, and Legacy Series: Thought Leadership and Brand Positioning

At Damac Group, we focused on establishing thought leadership and brand positioning through innovative content. We created the 'Empower Hour' video series, featuring fireside chats on exciting and interesting topics within Damac Group. This series allowed employees and external audiences to gain insights into our operations and corporate culture. Additionally, we launched 'DBate', an original podcast by Damac, to position the brand as an industry leader. Through this podcast, we discussed important topics and shared insights on the market and various business verticals, both regionally and globally. To further enhance our brand narrative, we developed the 'Legacy Series', a storytelling series showcasing the life of our founder and chairman while offering the world a glimpse into his journey and vision. These initiatives significantly enhanced our brand's credibility and attracted industry recognition.

A Legacy of Authenticity

To construct a personal brand that leaves a lasting legacy, it's crucial to reflect deeply on what you stand for and how you wish to be remembered. This process involves introspection and strategic action. Let's explore the steps needed to distill your essence into a personal brand that resonates and endures.

Step 1: Define Your Legacy

Defining your legacy involves identifying the core values and contributions you want to be remembered for. It's about understanding the impact you wish to have on the people and places you touch—be it in life, at a particular location, or within your workplace. This foundational step is about envisioning the 'footprint' you want to leave behind.

1. Reflect on Your Values: What principles guide your decisions and actions? Write them down.

2. Identify Your Contributions: Think about the skills, knowledge, and unique qualities you bring to your interactions and work.

3. Visualize Your Legacy: Imagine people discussing your impact. What would you like them to say?

Step 2: Discover Your Unique Fingerprint

Your 'fingerprint' is a metaphor for the unique mark you leave through your actions, creations, and influence. It's what differentiates you from others and encompasses your talents, your experiences, and the way you connect with the world.

1. Inventory Your Skills and Talents: List what you're good at, including 'soft skills' like empathy or leadership.

2. Assess Your Experiences: How have your experiences shaped you? Consider both professional and personal growth moments.

3. Define Your Connection Style: How do you engage with others? What makes your way of connecting special?

Step 3: Articulate Your Vision and Mission

Having a clear vision and mission guides your path and communicates your purpose to others. Your vision is the ultimate goal you aim for, while your mission is how you plan to get there.

1. Craft Your Vision Statement: Dream big. What do you want to achieve in the broader sense?

2. Develop Your Mission Statement: Be specific about how you intend to reach your vision. What actions will you take?

Step 4: Communicate Your Brand

Effectively communicating your personal brand involves consistently expressing your values, vision, and mission across various platforms and interactions. It's about ensuring that every touchpoint reflects your brand.

1. Choose Your Platforms Wisely: Determine where your audience spends their time and focus your efforts there.

2. Create Content that Reflects Your Brand: Whether it's blog posts, videos, or social media updates, ensure your content aligns with your legacy.

3. Engage Authentically: Interact with your community in a way that's true to your brand. Authenticity fosters deeper connections.

Step 5: Live Your Brand

A personal brand is not just what you say about yourself—it's what you do. Living your brand means making decisions and taking actions that align with your values, vision, and mission.

1. Align Actions with Values: Before making decisions, ask if they align with your core values.

2. Seek Opportunities that Fit Your Mission: Whether it's projects, collaborations, or career moves, choose paths that further your mission.

3. Reflect and Adjust: Regularly take stock of your actions and their impact. Adjust as needed to stay on course with your vision.

Remember, the most compelling personal brands are those lived with intention and purpose. Through reflection, discovery, and strategic action, you can ensure that your personal brand is a true reflection of who you are and the legacy you wish to leave.

Once you've discovered your unique fingerprint and defined the legacy you wish to leave, a profound sense of clarity emerges. This clarity influences how you see yourself and how you choose to present yourself to the world. While it's true that we cannot control how others perceive us, we *do* have significant control over the impression we create. This nuanced distinction is pivotal in personal branding and shaping your legacy.

PERCEPTION VS. IMPRESSION

Understanding the Difference:

- Perception is inherently subjective, filtered through others' experiences, biases, and expectations. It's the interpretation that people form about you based on various interactions and communications.
- Impression, on the other hand, is something you can craft through deliberate actions, communications, and presentations. It's the image you project and the vibes you give off intentionally.

How to Shape Your Impression

1. Consistency is Key:

Ensure that your actions, words, and presentations consistently reflect your core values and the lasting legacy you aim to build. Consistency reinforces your brand, making your intended impression more likely to stick.

2. Communicate with Purpose:

Every piece of content you create, every interaction you have, and every message you send should serve your larger mission and vision. Purposeful communication helps in creating a coherent and impactful impression.

3. Authentic Engagement:

Engage with your audience authentically. Authenticity builds trust and makes your intended impression more relatable and memorable. It's about showing your true self, not just a curated persona.

4. Be Mindful of Your Digital Footprint:

In today's Digital Age, much of your impression is formed online. Be mindful of your digital footprint—social media posts, blog articles, comments, and even the content you share. Ensure they align with the brand you're building.

5. Seek Feedback and Adapt:

While you can't control perception, you can learn from it. Seek feedback on how you're perceived and use this insight to refine the impression you aim to create. Be open to adjusting your approach to better align with your personal branding goals.

Embracing What You Can Control

The journey to understanding and shaping your personal brand is both introspective and outward-facing. It's about aligning your internal values and purpose with the external expression of your brand. By focusing on the elements within your control—the consistency of your actions, the purposefulness of your communication, your authenticity in engagements, and the mindfulness of your digital presence—you can craft an impression that closely aligns with your desired perception.

Remember, personal branding is not about manufacturing an image that's far removed from your true self; it's about strategically highlighting and sharing the aspects of yourself that resonate most with your values, your goals, and the legacy you wish to leave. In doing so, you navigate the complex interplay between perception and impression, steering your personal brand toward the legacy you envision.

Creating a strong first impression is vital in personal branding. It's your opportunity to communicate who you are, what you stand for, and what sets you apart from everyone else. This is crucial regardless of your current position, whether you're a C-suite executive, a student, or anywhere in between. Knowing how to market yourself effectively can open doors, create opportunities, and establish meaningful connections. Here's a personal branding exercise tailored to help you discover your niche and differentiate yourself:

Step 1: Identify Your Unique Value Proposition (UVP)

Your unique value proposition is a clear statement that describes the benefit of your offer, how you solve your audience's needs, and what distinguishes you from the competition. It's the cornerstone of making a memorable first impression.

1. List Your Skills and Strengths: Write down everything you're good at, particularly those skills that you enjoy and that others commend you for.

2. Identify Problems You Solve: Consider the challenges or needs of your target audience that you can address with your skills.

3. Distill Your Distinctiveness: What do you do better than anyone else? This could be a unique skill, an unusual combination of skills, or a unique perspective.

Step 2: Craft Your Elevator Pitch

An elevator pitch is a brief, persuasive speech that you use to spark interest in what you do. It should be concise and compelling, leaving the listener wanting more.

1. Integrate Your UVP: Start with your unique value proposition to immediately communicate your worth.

2. Keep it Short and Sweet: Aim for 30–60 seconds. Practice and refine it until it sounds natural.

3. End with a Question: This invites engagement and opens the floor for a deeper conversation.

Step 3: Build Your Personal Brand Statement

A personal brand statement is a one- or two-sentence phrase that sums up your brand. It's an extended version of your UVP that you can use on your resume, LinkedIn headline, or personal website.

1. Combine Your UVP and Aspirations: Incorporate what you do, who you do it for, and why you do it, along with where you're aiming to go in your career or personal development.

2. Make It Memorable: Use powerful, emotive words that resonate with your audience and reflect your personality.

Step 4: Visualize Your Brand

Personal branding isn't just verbal; it's also visual. The visual aspect of your brand should complement your brand statement and pitch, reinforcing the impression you wish to create.

1. Choose a Color Scheme: Colors can evoke emotions and convey your personality. Choose a palette that reflects the essence of your brand.

2. Select or Design a Logo: Even as an individual, a logo can be a powerful visual cue. (This could be as simple as a stylized version of your initials.)

3. Consistent Visuals Across Platforms: Ensure your LinkedIn profile, resume, personal website, and any other platforms have a consistent visual identity.

Step 5: Network and Engage

Building and maintaining a network is key to marketing yourself. Engage genuinely with others, both in your desired field and outside it.

1. Attend Industry Events: Whether virtual or in person, these can be great opportunities to meet others and practice your pitch.

2. Participate in Online Forums: Engage in discussions, offer advice, and share your insights.

3. Follow Up: After meetings or conversations, send a brief, personalized message to reinforce the connection and your brand.

By following these steps, you can develop a personal brand that not only makes a powerful first impression but also sets you apart in your niche. Remember, personal branding is an ongoing process of defining, articulating, and living your unique value proposition. Whether you're a C-suite executive looking to solidify your industry standing or a student starting your professional journey, understanding and effectively communicating your personal brand is indispensable.

Mastering the art of self-presentation and promoting your qualities isn't just about making a great first impression; it's about creating lasting connections that resonate with your personal and professional identity. This endeavor requires a deep dive into understanding, articulating, and living your personal brand.

Here's a comprehensive guide to developing and presenting your personal brand across various platforms and situations.

DEEP UNDERSTANDING OF YOUR BRAND

What You Stand For: Your personal brand is rooted in your core values—those principles that guide your life and work. Identifying these requires introspection. Consider the moments when you felt most fulfilled or proud. What values were you upholding? Integrity, creativity, reliability, and compassion are common core values, but it's essential to specify what these mean to you personally.

Creating Your Persona: Developing a persona is about crafting a narrative of who you are and who you aspire to be. This narrative isn't fiction; it's a structured way to present the authentic aspects of your character to the world. It encompasses your professional attributes, such as expertise in a particular field, and your personal qualities, like resilience or empathy. This persona should resonate with your target audience, whether they're potential employers, colleagues, or social acquaintances.

Messaging House: A messaging house organizes your key messages. The foundation is your mission—your 'why'. The pillars represent your offerings—your 'what'—such as skills, experiences, and the unique benefits you provide. The roof symbolizes your vision or ultimate goal. This structure helps ensure your messaging is consistent, focused, and impactful.

Artful Presentation of Yourself

Look and Feel: The visual elements of your brand—colors, style, and design—should mirror your personality and how you want to be perceived. Colors evoke emotions; for example, blue can signify trust and stability, while yellow may convey optimism and creativity. Extend this visual branding to your wardrobe, business cards, and online profiles to maintain consistency.

Character and Hobbies: Your interests and activities outside of work offer a glimpse into your personality, making your personal brand more relatable. Whether you're passionate about mountaineering, volunteer work, or playing a musical instrument, these hobbies can serve as conversation starters and demonstrate your multifaceted character.

Metaphorical Representations: Using metaphors like animals or books to describe yourself can offer insightful, memorable ways to convey your traits and values. If you're like a lion, perhaps you're a natural leader with a protective instinct. If you resonate with a particular book, it might reflect your journey, beliefs, or aspirations. These metaphors make abstract qualities tangible and relatable.

Inspirations: Discussing the people who inspire you reveals much about your aspirations and values. Whether it's a renowned leader, a mentor, or a family member, sharing why they inspire you can offer deeper insights into what drives you and the legacy you aim to build.

Implementing Your WHY, WHAT, HOW

- WHY: This is about connecting with your purpose. Reflect on the impact you want to have through your work and interactions. This purpose motivates you and guides your decisions.
- WHAT: Identify the tangible and intangible assets you bring. This includes not only your professional skills and achievements but also the personal strengths and experiences that inform your approach to challenges and opportunities.
- HOW: Your methods—how you accomplish your goals, interact with others, and overcome obstacles—reveal much about your character and work ethic. This could be your collaborative approach, your innovative problem-solving techniques, or your ability to inspire and motivate those around you.

Bringing Your Brand to Life

In Job Interviews: Use this platform to weave your personal brand narrative into your responses. Share stories that highlight your values, how you've applied your skills to achieve results, and the lessons you've learned. This approach transforms standard interview answers into compelling narratives that demonstrate your unique value proposition.

While Networking: Networking is about building relationships, not just exchanging business cards. Approach conversations with curiosity and a genuine interest in the other person. Seamlessly integrate aspects of your personal brand into these interactions by sharing relevant experiences, asking insightful questions, and offering help that aligns with your skills and interests.

In Social Settings: Social situations allow for a broader expression of your personal brand. This is an opportunity to show the more personal sides of your brand, like your humor, empathy, or other qualities that might not be front and center in professional settings.

Your personal brand is more than a marketing tool; it's a comprehensive expression of your identity, values, and aspirations. By carefully crafting and consistently living your personal brand, you ensure that every interaction—whether in a job interview, a networking event, or social gathering—reflects the authentic and unique individual you are. This not only helps you stand out but also fosters genuine connections that can enrich both your personal and your professional life.

Athletes are among the most visible personal brands globally, and many have transcended their sports careers to build powerful brands that impact business, philanthropy, fashion, and culture. Here are some top personal branding examples from athletes:

GLOBAL ATHLETES
WITH STRONG PERSONAL BRANDS

1. Cristiano Ronaldo – Soccer (Football)

- Brand Message: Cristiano Ronaldo's brand revolves around excellence, hard work, and fitness. He is known for his relentless pursuit of greatness, discipline, and peak performance, which is reflected in both his on-field success and off-field ventures.
- Social Media Power: Ronaldo is one of the most-followed athletes on social media, with over 500 million followers on Instagram. His brand is global, crossing borders and cultures, making him a sought-after partner for luxury and sports brands.
- Business Ventures: Ronaldo has built a business empire that includes his CR7 fashion line, hotels, and partnerships with brands like Nike. His image is synonymous with luxury, style, and peak physical condition.

2. LeBron James – Basketball

- Brand Message: LeBron James' personal brand emphasizes leadership, social impact, and athletic excellence. He has used his platform to speak on issues of social justice, equality, and education.
- Off-Court Impact: Beyond basketball, LeBron is known for his I PROMISE School, which he launched to help underprivileged children in his hometown. His media company, SpringHill Entertainment, has produced major film and TV projects, further extending his influence into entertainment.

- Business Ventures: LeBron's brand transcends basketball, with business interests that include part ownership of Liverpool FC, collaborations with Nike, and endorsements with major brands like Pepsi and Beats by Dre.

3. Serena Williams – Tennis

- Brand Message: Serena Williams' personal brand is built on empowerment, strength, and breaking barriers. She is not only one of the greatest athletes in history but also a cultural icon who advocates for gender equality and women's empowerment.
- Diverse Ventures: Serena has extended her brand into fashion with her Serena clothing line and into venture capital with Serena Ventures, which focuses on funding women and minority-owned businesses.
- Legacy of Advocacy: Serena's powerful voice in fighting for equal pay in tennis and advocating for diversity in sports and business has made her a global icon beyond her athletic achievements.

4. Tom Brady – American Football (NFL)

- Brand Message: Tom Brady's personal brand is centered on longevity, health, and peak performance. He's known for his commitment to a strict diet and fitness regimen, which has allowed him to perform at an elite level well into his 40s.
- Business Expansion: Brady has capitalized on his brand with his TB12 Sports line, offering fitness and wellness products, and his media company, 199 Productions, focusing on storytelling and content creation.

- Resilience and Leadership: Brady's personal brand focuses on leadership, resilience, and mental toughness, making him a respected figure not only in sports but in business and personal development circles.

5. David Beckham – Soccer (Football)

- Brand Message: David Beckham's personal brand is built on fashion, style, and global appeal. He was one of the first athletes to become a global celebrity outside of sports, known for his sense of style and family values.
- Business and Philanthropy: Beckham has parlayed his soccer fame into successful ventures in fashion, with his David Beckham Eyewear and partnerships with brands like H&M. He is also co-owner of Inter Miami CF, further solidifying his status as a global sports entrepreneur.
- Philanthropy: Beckham has been involved in numerous charitable causes, including his role as a UNICEF Goodwill Ambassador, which has elevated his brand as a humanitarian.

Middle East Athletes with Strong Personal Brands

1. Mohamed Salah – Soccer (Football)

- Brand Message: Salah's brand is centered on humility, philanthropy, and success. Despite being one of the world's best soccer players, he remains grounded and dedicated to giving back to his community.

- Philanthropy: Salah is known for his charitable efforts in his hometown of Nagrig, Egypt, where he has helped build schools, hospitals, and sports facilities. His humble personality and dedication to his roots make him a beloved figure not only in Egypt but across the Arab world.
- Global Influence: Salah's influence extends beyond soccer, making him a cultural ambassador for both Egypt and the Arab world. His presence in Europe has helped break down stereotypes and promote diversity.

2. Sheikh Mansour bin Zayed Al Nahyan – Horse Racing

- Brand Message: Sheikh Mansour is known for his deep passion for horse racing and investment in the global sport, making him a significant figure in the UAE's sports scene. His leadership and love for equestrian sports have helped elevate the UAE's reputation in the racing world.
- Legacy in Horse Racing: As a member of the Abu Dhabi royal family, Sheikh Mansour has been a key driver in promoting Arabian horse racing globally. His sponsorship of events and investment in high-quality breeding has made him a brand icon in the sport.

3. Omar Abdulrahman – Soccer (Football)

- Brand Message: Omar Abdulrahman, known as "Amoory", is one of the most skilled footballers in the Middle East. His brand is built around creativity, skill, and passion for football, earning him a loyal fanbase across the Gulf.

- Icon of Emirati Football: As one of the UAE's best-known players, Abdulrahman represents the rise of football in the region, and his brand is centered around sportsmanship, creativity, and technical ability on the field.

Key Takeaways from Athlete Personal Branding

- Authenticity: Many of these athletes succeed because their brand reflects who they are both on and off the field.
- Expansion Beyond Sports: Athletes like LeBron James and Serena Williams have used their fame to build businesses, engage in philanthropy, and influence culture, expanding their brand beyond their athletic achievements.
- Global Reach: Athletes like Cristiano Ronaldo and Mohamed Salah have created brands that transcend geographic and cultural boundaries, making them global icons.
- Social Media Power: Athletes increasingly use platforms like Instagram and Twitter to build their brands, engaging with fans directly and creating content that aligns with their values and personality.

Both Mel Robbins and Tony Robbins are powerful examples of personal branding in the self-development and motivational space. While they share similarities in their fields, they have distinct approaches and personal brand elements that have contributed to their global success.

Mel Robbins – Author, Speaker, and Life Coach

- Brand Message: Mel Robbins has built her personal brand around practical, science-backed advice to help people overcome personal struggles, build confidence, and take action in their lives. Her message emphasizes simplicity and actionable steps for personal growth.
- Signature Concept: Mel's brand skyrocketed with her "5 Second Rule", a simple tool to push oneself to take immediate action. This concept is central to her brand, making her highly relatable, as it focuses on overcoming procrastination, fear, and doubt in everyday life.
- Authenticity: Mel Robbins is known for her candidness, sharing personal stories of struggle, including financial difficulties, anxiety, and career setbacks. This openness and vulnerability make her approachable, especially to women and individuals seeking practical advice in everyday scenarios.
- Content Strategy: Mel leverages platforms like YouTube, Instagram, and podcasts to reach her audience. She focuses on real-world advice and inspiration, often sharing motivational tips, behind-the-scenes glimpses into her life, and advice on overcoming anxiety and achieving goals.

KEY PERSONAL BRANDING ELEMENTS

- Practical, no-nonsense advice.
- Focus on overcoming fear and taking immediate action.
- Relatable storytelling and vulnerability.
- Strong presence on social media platforms.

Tony Robbins – Life Coach, Author, and Philanthropist

- Brand Message: Tony Robbins' personal brand is built around empowering people to achieve extraordinary levels of success in all aspects of life, including business, relationships, and personal fulfilment. His message revolves around breaking through limits and maximizing human potential.
- Signature Events: Tony Robbins is known for his high-energy, transformative events like "Unleash the Power Within" and "Date with Destiny." These events are central to his brand, creating a sense of community and immersion in his teachings. His immersive approach differentiates him from other speakers.
- Influence on Leadership and Wealth: Unlike Mel, Tony's brand has a broader focus, including leadership training, wealth management, and high-performance coaching. He is seen as a mentor to top CEOs, athletes, and leaders globally, further expanding his influence.
- Content and Outreach: Tony has a diversified content strategy, including bestselling books like *Awaken the Giant Within* and podcasts. He has built a strong brand ecosystem that includes seminars, coaching, and digital content, positioning him as a global authority on self-improvement.

Key Personal Branding Elements:

- High energy, life-changing events with a focus on mindset transformation.
- Deep focus on success and financial mastery, coaching high achievers.
- Strong presence in leadership and performance coaching.

- Expansive content from books to live events, covering multiple life domains.

Here are some top personal branding examples globally and in the Middle East, illustrating how individuals have effectively built strong and recognizable brands:

Global Personal Branding Examples

1. Oprah Winfrey – Media Mogul and Philanthropist

Oprah has built her brand around authenticity, empathy, and self-empowerment. She created an empire from her talk show, expanding into a multi-platform media business, philanthropy, and a global brand. Her brand is synonymous with trust, personal growth, and positive impact.

2. Elon Musk – CEO of Tesla and SpaceX

Known for his audacious goals, innovative mindset, and a strong presence on social media, Elon Musk's personal brand is closely tied to visionary leadership and pushing the boundaries of technology. His Twitter activity helps shape his brand, making him a relatable yet bold public figure.

3. Richard Branson – Founder of Virgin Group

Branson's adventurous spirit, combined with his unconventional business practices, has helped him craft a personal brand that is fun, risk-taking, and approachable. His strong connection to the Virgin brand makes him a global entrepreneurial icon.

4. Gary Vaynerchuk – Entrepreneur, Author, & Public Speaker

Gary Vee has built a personal brand around hustle culture, entrepreneurship, and digital marketing. His straight-talking, motivational content has made him one of the most well-known voices in the business world, leveraging platforms like Instagram, YouTube, and podcasts.

Middle East Personal Branding Examples

1. Huda Kattan – Founder of Huda Beauty

Huda Kattan has become a beauty industry powerhouse by building a personal brand around makeup artistry, authenticity, and entrepreneurship. She leveraged social media, particularly Instagram and YouTube, to grow Huda Beauty into a global brand while keeping her personal story at the center of her brand.

2. Sheikha Bodour Al Qasimi – Chairperson of Sharjah Book Authority

Known for her leadership in publishing, culture, and education, Sheikha Bodour has built a personal brand around literacy, cultural diplomacy, and empowering women. Her advocacy for global cultural dialogue has elevated her as a key figure in the UAE and internationally.

3. Queen Rania of Jordan – Queen of Jordan and Humanitarian

Queen Rania's brand revolves around education, children's welfare, and social justice. Through her public engagements and digital presence, she has established herself as a global voice for progressive values and humanitarian efforts, balancing her royal duties with advocacy work.

These individuals have crafted their personal brands through authenticity, leadership, and a strategic alignment between their personal values and public presence. Their influence extends across industries, making them strong examples of effective personal branding.

CONCLUSION

Living a Purpose

For those who have a message, creating a personal brand is important. The act of putting valuable content, narrative, and messaging out into the world for others to discover becomes your legacy.

You're leaving behind assets, knowledge, and words that will eventually influence someone who watched your reel, saw your post, or read your tweet. They'll take that and do something with it, which will make a difference.

Personal branding is important, because it's who you are. You're not simply what you do, it's how you walk the talk, and how you show up as empathetic, driven, inspirational, and responsible. It will show in the way you:

- Run an organization
- Create policies and procedures
- Treat, recognize, and motivate your people

- Grow your business and make deals
- Serve your customers
- Positively impact your vendors, community, environment, and planet.

Do you do business ethically? What are your values? What do you stand for? All of these are important. What are organizations made up of? What are countries made up of? *People.*

It's all about people. Eventually it comes down to how you build connections, from the head to the heart and back to the head.

We need to have a human-to-human connection. We always talk about B2B and B2C, but can we talk about H2H as well?

The future is about connecting H2H.

AUTHOR BIO

Mariam Farag is a seasoned communications and branding leader with over 20 years of experience across sectors such as real estate, hospitality, technology, retail, media, academia, and non-profit. Renowned for her expertise in humanizing brands, she specializes in strategic communications, digital media, and impactful storytelling. Mariam has a proven track record of managing global initiatives, fostering thought leadership, and driving meaningful engagement through innovative campaigns that align with business and societal goals.

Her efforts have been widely acknowledged, including being honored with the Humanitarian of the Year Award at the C3 Summit during the UN General Assembly in New York City. In addition, she has received recognition as a top achiever in her field. On a personal front, Mariam values humanity and positivity. Committed to sparking conversations that build genuine relationships, she dedicates her time, attention, and love to creating a sustainable, empowered future generation. Through her workshops on personal branding, public speaking, and storytelling for impact, she continues to inspire meaningful change while contributing to sustainability, inclusivity, and community-building.

Get in Touch:

http://Mariamfarag.com

@mariamfaragofficial

Mariam Farag

MariamFarag_04

For keynotes, media and business inquiries, please contact: mariam.farag@humanizingbrands.com

WORKS CITED

Airbnb (n.d.). *Store website.* https://www.airbnb.com/

Bogwasi, T. (2023, March 27). Brand Storytelling in 2024: The Latest Statistics and Trends. *The blog.* https://www.blog.thebrandshopbw. com/brand-storytelling-statistics-and-trends/

DAMAC Originals. (2022–23). *DBate* [Audio podcast]. DAMAC Properties. https://podcasts.apple.com/au/podcast/dbate/ id1650569841/

Elnakoury, N. (Director). (2012). MBC Hope [Television campaign]. MBC Channel.

Gallegos, J. (2020, January 16). 46 Mind-Blowing Stats About User-Generated Content. *Tint.* https://www.tintup.com/blog/user-generated-content-stats-study/

Great Place to Work. (n.d.). *Certification.* https://www.greatplacetowork. com/solutions/certification

Green Thumbs Garden Supply. (n.d.). *Store website.* https://greenthumb gardensupplymt.com/

IKEA. (n.d.). *Store website.* https://www.ikea.com/

MBC (n.d.). *Television network.* https://www.mbc.net/

MBC Academy (n.d.). *Company website.* https://www.mbcacademy. me/ar/home

Murray, D. (Producer), & Miller, J.J. (Director). (2019). I am Richard Pryor [Television broadcast]. Paramount Network.

Power Reviews. (n.d.). How User-Generated Content Impacts Conversion: 2023 Edition. https://www.powerreviews.com/how-ugc-impacts-conversion-2023/

TechGlobal (n.d.). *Store website.* https://techglobal.com/

TechStars (n.d.). *Company website.* http://www.techstars.com/

.

www.ingramcontent.com/pod-product-compliance
Lightning Source LLC
Chambersburg PA
CBHW030507210326
41597CB00013B/827